So Small a World

Frontispiece: Not even the north or south polar regions can now escape pollution by man, as is shown by this picture of Adélie penguins at Cape Hallett, near the joint United States–New Zealand Antarctic research station

Guy Mountfort

So Small
a World

Foreword by
HRH The Prince Philip,
Duke of Edinburgh KG KT

CHARLES SCRIBNER'S SONS
NEW YORK

1 3 5 7 9 11 13 15 17 19   I/C 20 18 16 14 12 10 8 6 4 2

Printed in Great Britain

Library of Congress Catalog Card Number 74–14156
ISBN 0–684–14119–1

To the pioneers

*whose lonely work for conservation enriched
my travels and whose example taught me
that even one man's efforts to save what
remains of the beauty of the natural world
can be worthwhile.*

Contents

Illustrations

All illustrations are by the author, except Plate 1(b) by Barnaby's Picture Library; Plate 2(b) by Eric Hosking; Plate 8(b) by Norman Myers, W.W.F.; Plate 10(b) by H. J. Frith; 15(b) by World Wildlife Fund. The frontispiece and Plates 11(b), 14(b), 15(a), 16(a) and (b) are by George Holton.

Foreword

by HRH The Prince Philip,
Duke of Edinburgh KG KT

All over this shrinking world more and more people are beginning to appreciate the beauties and wonders of the natural world. Everything from quite small Zoological Gardens in the hearts of great cities, to the wide open spaces of the great National Parks of America, Asia and Africa is thronged with people anxious to see the animals. This is splendid, because only massive public interest and sympathy can keep rare animal species going.

The trouble is that not enough people have been able to find out about the problems and the pressures which wild populations are having to face in a world of exploding human populations and all the consequences of the exploitation of natural resources and rapidly developing industries.

A very great deal has been achieved by such dedicated people as Guy Mountfort, but the situation really is critical, as he makes very clear in this penetrating book. I hope you will enjoy it and I hope it will give an added interest to your next visit to the Zoo, or Safari Park or, if you are really lucky, to one of the great National Parks overseas.

Buckingham Palace

Author's Preface

For one reason or another it has been my good fortune, as an amateur naturalist, to spend much of my life travelling around the world. At different times I have lived for a total of thirteen years in countries other than my own. I take no particular credit for this, nor pose as an explorer. It just so happened that my personal interests, my business career, or the army, took me abroad. Organized sight-seeing, however, holds few attractions for me. Since childhood I have always preferred to see what lies beyond the highways.

Half a million miles of travel on liaison duties with the allied armies took me through the hinterlands of five continents and to many remote islands which during the War had assumed temporary strategic importance. These journeys, though occasionally attended by unpleasant events, always rewarded me with a broader understanding of the natural world. After the War, my travels became more selective and the number of countries I had visited passed the hundred mark. The devastation caused by the War, and the far greater damage to the environment brought about by technology during the following decades, instilled in me a deep conviction of the need to save what little remained of unspoilt wilderness and its rapidly disappearing wildlife.

The formation of the World Wildlife Fund, in which I took part, provided the means by which I could translate my interest into action. Since then I have had the satisfaction of helping to create national parks and wildlife reserves in a number of different countries. The preparatory work, which involved the organization of nine strenuous exploratory expeditions, was richly rewarding. On each occasion I was accompanied by a team of distinguished specialists in the various scientific disciplines, from whom I learned a great deal. Equally rewarding was the discovery in many countries of people who shared my enthusiasm for saving wildlife from extinction. My admiration is boundless for these hard-working men and women of every nationality who, despite local apathy and bureaucratic frustrations, continue to achieve miracles by sheer perseverance. Some of the dedicated pioneers, such as John Owen, Ian Grimwood and John Blower, have made contributions of incalculable value to conservation in Africa, South America and Asia. Their work deserves to be as well known as that of the great international figures in conservation such as Sir Peter Scott, Gerardo Budowski, Sir Julian Huxley, Ira Gabrielson and Max Nicholson.

The struggle to equate the development of human progress with the protection of the global environment and the ever more rapid depletion of natural resources, can only be resolved by wise compromise. Economic growth and social progress cannot indefinitely be pursued at the expense of the quality of life on earth. To continue such a policy can only widen the gulf between the haves and the have-nots and lead ultimately to conflict. Development must be fair to all and must at every stage include an element for the improvement of the human condition, or it will be useless. If we are to survive the pressures of the next century, the land and oceans must remain fully productive, our fresh water and our air free of harmful pollution. Wilderness and wildlife must be allowed to survive, not merely because nature fills a vital need for beauty in our lives, nor merely because animals have a right to life, but because man and nature are totally interdependent and the products of the same evolutionary process. The diversity of life on earth is our richest asset. We destroy it at our peril. It is not sufficient that the United Nations and 130 governments are now pledged to protect the environment. The task is one which can only succeed if every individual feels personally involved and plays his part by restraint and by opening his mind to the realities of human survival in the twenty-first century.

We have many options open to us for the uses to which we

put our remaining undeveloped land. It can be left intact in its natural state for scientific or educational use; for development as a tourist attraction, a national park or a wildlife reserve; for the controlled harvesting of its timber or wildlife on a sustained yield basis; for farming or tree plantations; or it can be stripped of its vegetation and wildlife for mining, or industrial or urban development. Obviously if the last mentioned uses are chosen, the door is closed for ever on the other options, all of which are capable of alternative conversion at the wish of future generations. All too often, either for lack of forethought or more frequently by deliberate decision to obtain a short-term benefit regardless of the future, we deny our descendants any freedom of choice.

Only if the decision makers, and this usually means politicians, can be taught the essential principles of conservation are options likely to be kept open. There is nothing mysterious or difficult to comprehend about these principles. Perhaps the greater difficulty lies in the inability of the decision makers to put the problems of the future on the same plane as the always pressing need for quick results to solve the problems of today.

This book represents a purely personal view of the changing natural world as I have seen it on my travels. Though some of the conclusions expressed may sound pessimistic, I am by nature an optimist. Conservation is now making undeniable progress and some of its successes are described. If the facts were better known about the terrifying rapidity with which the natural world is being destroyed, this progress could be accelerated. An informed public opinion is, after all, the most powerful weapon in fighting government apathy and vested interests. As Kurt Waldheim, Secretary-General of the United Nations, said of human progress in relation to conservation: 'It cannot reach its goals without the whole world's backing.'

It is later than we think. And we can no longer pretend that time is on our side. From the Bronze Age to the Industrial Revolution men lived in partnership with nature. From then onward, in the words of G. M. Trevelyan: 'Man armed with the machine could not help destroying beauty, whatever the work to which he put his hand.' Modern man was born atrophied, but with the help of conservationists we are learning what we have lost and the importance of trying to save what remains of our natural heritage. Painfully we are recovering the love of nature and of beauty, which for centuries was the hallmark of civilized man.

I am grateful to Messrs Collins Ltd, Messrs Hutchinson Ltd and Messrs David & Charles Ltd for permission to include in this volume some brief extracts from three of my earlier books. I also thank my friends Eric Hosking and George Holton for permitting me to use some of their excellent photographs and Dr Harry Frith for allowing me to include a picture and information from his remarkable book on the mallee-fowl.

G.M.

I Politics and the Naturalist

By the nature of their work, naturalists tend to be internationally minded, because their subject matter can rarely be studied in the confines of neatly man-made political boundaries. They are therefore impatient of the restrictions which so often prevent them from obtaining information from countries which are suspicious of foreigners. That these suspicions can be dispelled, however, was demonstrated when I was invited with the late James Fisher in 1956 to the first ornithological congress of the USSR in Leningrad. We were apparently the first Englishmen so honoured. The meetings were at the Academy of Sciences and 400 Russians were present, most of whom, I was surprised to find, spoke quite serviceable English, though very few had ever been outside their country.

In addressing the assembly, I reminded the Russians that migratory birds did not recognize political frontiers and that they could only be studied satisfactorily by international co-operation, which should include a free exchange of published papers. This brought a more than merely polite round of applause and afterwards also a flood of much-needed Russian ornithological literature to Britain. Professor Erwin Stresemann of Germany, who had been invited to the congress, followed me with a proposal that the currently very advanced Russian programme of faunistic investigations should be combined with that of other countries in the production of a distribution census embracing the entire palaearctic region. This, too, was accepted with applause. At the inevitable banquet which terminated the congress, James Fisher, Erwin Stresemann and I were fêted in true Russian manner. At 3 a.m., by which time the ever-flowing vodka had taken full effect, one of the Russian scientists made a speech, declaring amid cheers, 'We are not communists or capitalists here — we are ornithologists!' Whereupon we were rushed upon by the assembled delegates and tossed six times high among the ornate chandeliers as a gesture of international brotherhood.

There are still many countries all over the world where the sight of a man carrying binoculars and a camera arouses suspicion. If he is outside the officially prescribed tourist limits, he will probably find himself under surveillance and being asked to produce his credentials. My first experience of this xenophobia was in 1935, when I was living in France. Not far from my house near St Germain, where the Seine doubles back in a long loop, there was a tract of marshland much favoured by a variety of interesting birds. It was my habit during the nesting season to cycle to this pleasant spot for an hour's bird-watching before breakfast. Between six and seven in the morning I rarely saw anyone else there, except for an occasional peasant trudging off to work in the fields. I was therefore more than a little surprised one morning, when I was sitting happily under a bush watching some nesting wagtails through my binoculars, to be suddenly challenged by a large, red-bearded gendarme who had approached unheard behind me.

Brusquely he asked for my *carte d'identité* and demanded an explanation for my presence. Somewhat amused, I led him to the carefully concealed nest and parted the grasses to reveal the four gaping nestlings. I explained that they were young *bergeronettes printanières*. He looked unimpressed and pointed across the river accusingly.

'I am reliably informed,' he said, 'that you are here every morning at sunrise, examining the military installations of St Germain with your binoculars. You will accompany me to the gendarmerie.' Sure enough, beyond my line of sight to the inoffensive wagtails, were the long ramparts on the high bluff of St Germain. My explanation falling on deaf ears, we cycled sedately to the police station. My papers were carefully examined by the desk sergeant, who obviously shared his colleague's disbelief that anyone in his right mind could be interested in watching insignificant small birds. I had often been told that the French loved birds, providing that they were delicately cooked. He was, however, courteous and puzzled rather than suspicious.

'Do you know anyone of substance who can vouch for your presence *under a bush*, at so strange an hour?' he enquired.

It was barely seven o'clock and few of my French friends were early risers. I gave him the telephone number of a member of the Société Française d'Ornithologie, to which I belonged. In deference to my friend, who held a senior appointment in one of the ministries, I suggested that he should not be called until half past seven. Impressed by the mention of a ministry, the sergeant sent for coffee and we chatted pleasantly until the call came through. My friend satisfied the sergeant that I was merely an eccentric Englishman, whose interest in ornithology had nothing to do with espionage, and we parted with handshakes all round.

A more amusing incident, this time in the British political sphere, occurred after I had returned from the second explorations of the Coto Doñana, in Southern Spain, which later resulted in the creation of the Coto Doñana National Park. It had been a fairly large expedition, requiring a considerable weight of stores and equipment. As our finances had been slender, Field Marshal Lord Alanbrooke, who was one of our cinematographers, had offered to ask Admiral of the Fleet Earl Mountbatten if some of the heavy gear could be carried as far as Gibraltar in a naval vessel. To my delight this was readily agreed. Unfortunately, news of the generous co-operation of the Royal Navy leaked out and it soon became a political issue. The prominent Socialist Mr Emanuel Shinwell (now Lord Shinwell), a jealous guardian of official rectitude and never one to miss an opportunity of embarrassing his opponents, put down a question in the House of Commons. Tipped off by a friendly press correspondent, I was in the public gallery when he rose to speak. The Hansard report of 29th April 1958 provides a delightful example of British democracy at work. The question read:

'Mr. Shinwell asked the Parliamentary Secretary to the Admiralty what facilities were provided by his Department for the transport of stores and equipment for a private bird-watching expedition conducted by Mr. Guy Mountfort; what Admiralty vessel was used for this purpose; what was the amount paid for these services; and whether his consent was obtained for this transaction.'

In reply the Parliamentary Secretary made clear that the Fleet Auxiliary, H.M.S. *Fort Dunvegan*, had been returning to the Mediterranean in ballast; that there was no demand for the space available; that a proper handling charge had been made; and that the arrangement had received his approval. It was perfectly in accordance with custom, he said, for the Admiralty to provide facilities for a serious expedition of an international character, the reports of which would be of value, providing that no displacement of official freight was involved.

When another M.P., Mr George Chetwynd, interjected the question, 'Are we to assume that the birds concerned were wrens?' (a play on the popular name for the Women's Royal Naval Service) the House dissolved in laughter, in which the discomfited Mr Shinwell could not refrain from joining. The matter was nicely rounded off by a comment from Mr James Callaghan that the action by the Royal Navy had been 'a perfectly normal and good piece of public relations'.

My next brush with politics was of a potentially more serious nature. In 1960 I led the first of two expeditions to study the wildlife and conservation problems of the Danube, first in Bulgaria and later in Hungary. The timing was not well chosen in relation to the growing tension between East and West over the development of atomic weaponry; but I had received an invitation from the Bulgarian authorities which I felt I could not refuse without giving offence. Moreover this was the first opportunity since the War for a British group to study the ecological changes which had undoubtedly occurred in the valley of the Danube.

We arrived in Sofia on the 15th of May and were met by the President of the Committee for Cultural Relations and other officials, who assured us that all local arrangements for the expedition had been made. Nevertheless, I began to feel uneasy when, by the evening of the second day, there was still no sign of our promised vehicles. We had, however, completed the necessary round of official visits and were royally entertained that night by the resident British Minister, Mr (now Sir) Anthony Lambert. Being a very skilled ornithologist, he was able to provide us with valuable information concerning the regions we planned to visit.

With breakfast next morning came news of the international uproar over the shooting down by Russia of the American U-2 'spy-plane' and the collapse of the Big Four conference in Paris. The Bulgarian press was full of prophecies of the outbreak of World War III. All the officials with whom we had been dealing immediately became 'not available' when I called them and we found ourselves isolated. I had visions of my group being caught behind the Iron Curtain and I hurried back to the Legation. Here I found the Minister completely unruffled. He had seen it all before and counselled patience. The day dragged on without my being able to contact a single Bulgarian concerned with the expedition. But in the evening the Minister came in smiling, with the news that the authorities had released the vehicles and that we could begin the expedition as planned the following morning. How he had achieved this at a time of such tension I will never know, but my esteem for British diplomacy soared to a new peak.

Our work in Bulgaria was completed without further incident and was very enjoyable, though we were aware of being kept under discreet surveillance in certain areas. When we were working in the sun-scorched Dobruja plains, I felt sorry for the little man in the shiny serge suit who had to sit from dawn to dusk in a sizzling-hot Russian car on a hill-top. However, the local peasants everywhere gave us enthusiastic welcomes and I had to make many speeches in village halls and drink innumerable toasts in fiery *slivova*. Thousands of western tourists now enjoy the superb sand beaches of the Black Sea coast, but in most of the areas we visited we were the first people from a capitalist country to be seen since the War.

Our photographer, Eric Hosking, had an amusing experience

with an inquisitive sentry when he was in a hide photographing some birds nesting in a chalk cliff near Cape Kaliakra. Without warning, he was suddenly prodded through the back of the hide by a bayonet. With a cry of anguish he scrambled out to find an armed sentry with a fierce guard-dog, which seemed intent on tearing the hide to pieces. There followed one of those entrancing 'conversations' in which we had all become adept, neither side comprehending a single word spoken by the other. Finding himself getting nowhere, Eric resourcefully fished in his pocket and produced the only paper he could find. It was a cable from his wife. The sentry studied this thoughtfully, saluted respectfully and withdrew.

The following year, when we were exploring the Danube in Hungary, I wondered whether the staunchly pro-Russian government officials were aware of the part I had played in organizing the sending of food and clothing to refugees at the time of the revolution of 1956. If they were, it apparently did not affect the kindness with which we were everywhere treated by the Hungarians. Budapest was still heavily scarred by the gun-fire which had been used to suppress the revolution and the event was still all too fresh in the memories of most of the people we met. I had, however, warned my colleagues against being drawn into political discussion of any kind.

A very agreeable young man was provided by the authorities to act as interpreter during our stay in Hungary. He spoke English fluently and helped us in many ways. Once we were alone, however, he was embarrassingly outspoken against the government and claimed to have taken an active part in the revolution. I became increasingly uneasy about his frequent attempts to encourage first one and then another of us to discuss politics. Some years later I was not altogether surprised when his name appeared in press reports of the arrest of a British businessman in Hungary on charges of espionage. The *agent provocateur* who led him into the hands of the secret police was our friendly young 'interpreter'.

Hungary is still one of Europe's most beautiful countries and our work took us to some of its regions which have remained totally unmarred by modernity of any kind. One of these was a tiny village in the Mátra Mountains near Gyöngyöspata. Here we found a long procession approaching a small fourteenth-century church set among ancient trees. First came small boys in crimson cassocks and white surplices, swinging censers, then eight maidens in white, carrying the shrine of the Virgin under an embroidered canopy. A venerable priest followed, leading perhaps fifty women in the full glory of traditional Hapsburg costumes — high lace headdresses, richly embroidered short jackets over tight velvet bodices, bell-shaped skirts billowing out over ten or twelve layers of stiffly pleated petticoats, and white cotton stockings with buckled black shoes. No two costumes were alike in their vivid colours and decorations. Finally came the men, in black broadcloth and wide-brimmed hats, carrying religious banners. Everyone was singing, as only the people of the land of Bartók and Kodály can sing, as though music comes as spontaneously as breathing.

Our cinematographer and sound recorder instantly had their equipment in action to record this superb event. When the procession had entered the church, they were sitting in their car when a plainclothes policeman ordered them peremptorily to get out. He announced that he was confiscating the film and taking them into custody. Our young interpreter hurried up and, after a discussion which we could not follow, told us it had all been a mistake. It just so happened, he said, that the villagers had been singing a hymn which had been 'proscribed by the authorities'. Asked what was wrong with the hymn, he replied apologetically that it was regarded as subversive, because of the words in the refrain 'Mother of God, save Thy Hungarian people'. But, he added, freedom of worship was, of course, assured by the Hungarian Constitution, under the agreement between Church and State.

In 1963 we were briefly involved in a rather more dramatic incident when we were conducting a wildlife survey at the invitation of King Hussein in Jordan. Our Land-Rovers had taken a bad beating while working in the lava desert near the Azraq oasis and I decided to take them back to Amman for attention. We were drinking beer on the terrace of the old

Philadelphia Hotel opposite the Roman forum, when we heard a number of shots. People began running, the young towards the sound of the firing and the old away from it. Shortly afterwards several army vehicles raced past, full of armed soldiers and we heard the sound of shouting and the chanting of slogans. The commotion then died down and we thought no more about it. Next day the papers carried news of rioting which, stimulated by pro-Nasser agents, had broken out simultaneously in Amman, Jericho, Jerusalem and Nablus. Reports in the British press, which we did not see until our return to England, were grossly exaggerated and caused considerable alarm among our wives. Screaming headlines claimed that machine-guns and tanks had mown down hundreds of civilians, whereas I was told by the Jordanian Prime Minister that the total number killed throughout the country had been only seven. The Prime Minister later told me how the rioting in Amman had been stopped. King Hussein had dashed from the Basman Palace in his open sports car, unescorted, to the scene of the shooting. Forcing his car between the rioters and the soldiers, who had fired warning shots over the heads of the crowd, he appealed for calm. The astonished assembly broke into spontaneous cheering and the incident was over. Not a word of this courageous action appeared in the British press.

The wide publicity given to the opening of the Azraq Desert National Park by King Hussein, which followed our work in Jordan, led to my being invited by President Ayub Khan of Pakistan to conduct a similar study of the conservation problems of that country. In 1966 and 1969 I therefore found myself again involved in organizing large-scale expeditions. Apart from the disputed cease-fire line on the Azad-Kashmir border and the Gilgit frontier with China, we had no restrictions on our movements and had a thoroughly rewarding time. We were, however, appalled by the losses of wildlife which had occurred, particularly in West Pakistan. By nature the Pakistani is a born *shikari* and the excessive pressure of hunting since the Second World War had been disastrous to all the larger mammals and birds. The skin traders had also taken a terrible toll of all fur-bearing animals and large reptiles such as the crocodilians, monitor lizards and big snakes, particularly the pythons which control Pakistan's dangerously large populations of rats.

One of our first recommendations to the Pakistan government was the obvious need to overhaul the very inadequate hunting laws and to introduce at least a temporary ban on the killing of all endangered species of wildlife. Understandably, this led to a great outcry from the less responsible hunters and skin traders. Although strongly supported by the government and conservationists in Pakistan, I found myself being attacked in letters to the press by one or two leading hunters, who claimed that our census of endangered species was inaccurate and that there were still plenty of game animals to be shot. These comments had little general support, however, and, with the President's backing, new legislation was introduced to protect wildlife and to create a number of new reserves.

After I returned to England I learned that one of the leading hunters in Pakistan was spreading stories that my work there had been a cover for espionage and that I had in reality been working for the Central Intelligence Agency of the United States. As a further embroidery to this tale, it was added that while working in Jordan I had been spying for the Israeli army. Spy fever and dislike of the C.I.A. are, of course, commonplace in many countries; but having worked so hard, and on a voluntary basis, for both Pakistan and Jordan, I was very distressed by these reports. However, I was advised to ignore them and I am glad to say that they did not affect the programme of conservation in Pakistan, which under President Bhutto is still continuing to expand.

With the help of the World Wildlife Fund, Pakistan has created a number of very promising new reserves, in which many of the now rare indigenous animal species are slowly beginning to recover. One of them, the Lal Suhanra Reserve, provides an admirable example of the kind of co-operative international effort which can be achieved by the World Wildlife Fund. Negotiations to create the reserve were conducted during my first expedition. It is a combination of marshes which shelter a wide variety of resident and migratory water-fowl and a tract of desert and degraded savanna once populated by numerous blackbuck and chinkara gazelles. Not very far from here, in 1886, the last of Pakistan's tigers was shot; what is now desert had then been covered with extensive thorn forest. As blackbuck are now almost extinct throughout the country, a breeding herd was obtained for the reserve through the American Appeal of the W.W.F., as a donation from one of the big Texan ranches, where these beautiful animals were introduced some years ago and are now more numerous than in their native Asia. The herd was successfully flown the 13,000 miles to Lal Suhanra where, under skilful management, it has begun to multiply. The heavy cost of fencing the large reserve was contributed by the Dutch Appeal. From the British Appeal came a breeding stock of the very rare marbled teal, raised and donated by Sir Peter Scott's Wildfowl Trust at Slimbridge. These uniquely marked little ducks occur as winter migrants on one or two of the *jheels* in Pakistan and it is hoped that they will become established as a breeding species in the safety of Lal Suhanra. Plans are now being discussed for the re-introduction of other once indigenous animals, such as the gavial, a long-snouted, fish-eating crocodilian which was once common in the backwaters of the Indus valley.

Another highly successful outcome of my expedition was the establishment of the Kalabagh Reserve in the Salt Range. These rugged, sun-scorched mountains are the last refuge of the Punjab urial, a beautiful mountain sheep with massive, curled horns. It is related to the Shapu sheep of the western Himalayas. The Salt Range is in the domain of the Nawab of Kalabagh, who for some years was Governor of West Pakistan. We spent several days in his beautiful rest-house, beside his walled palace on the bank of the Indus. To my delight, the Nawab readily agreed to my suggestion that the Salt Range habitat of the Punjab urial should become a fully protected reserve under the auspices of the World Wildlife Fund. It became, in fact, the first of Pakistan's new reserves. Today it represents a fine object lesson in the harnessing of private enterprise to a national conservation effort, for the property still belongs to the Nawab of Kalabagh, although administered in the national interest. When I last visited it, the urial population stood at about 500 animals, living in perfect equilibrium with their environment. Moreover, benefiting from the eagle-eyed protection provided by the fierce Kuttak Pathan guards, the reserve had attracted a considerable number of chinkara gazelles from the surrounding desert to reside in the foothills, where they were completely safe from hunters. The Nawab, alas, was killed in a shooting affray soon after my first visit, but the reserve continues to flourish under the care of his elder son, Malik Muzaffar Khan.

The most exciting discovery by our expeditions was that the unique western Tragopan pheasant was not, as previously believed, extinct. A fresh skin was found at Gilgit. But, alas, politics intervened. We were not permitted to explore its reported breeding area, which was near the snow-line right on the Azad-Kashmir cease-fire line!

2 The Godforsaken Island

During the War my military duties with the allied armies enabled me to visit many remote parts of the world which I might otherwise never have seen. One of these was the island of Bougainville, in the Solomons. General Sturdee, who commanded the Australian forces in New Guinea and Papua, sent me to examine the logistical problems of a pack howitzer unit which was currently engaging the Japanese in the mountainous hinterland of Bougainville. Accordingly, at dawn the following morning, I hitch-hiked a ride on an American Air Force Dakota from the General's palm-thatched headquarters camp at Lae and, after swinging in a wide arc over the Owen Stanley Range, headed north-east across the deep blue Solomon Sea. Half an hour later the 10,000-foot green mountains of Bougainville, capped with piled-up cumulus clouds, appeared on the horizon, gleaming like emeralds topped with whipped cream.

We landed on a rough airstrip near Torokina, a small settlement which was little more than a name on a map. Here I breakfasted in an open corrugated-iron shelter with a group of sun-bronzed Australian officers. One, an artilleryman, was to take me up to the forward gun positions.

'It's very quiet up there now,' he said. 'You'll enjoy the ride and with a bit of luck we'll make it before sundown.' I was to realize later what he meant by this cryptic remark.

As we loaded our bed-rolls into the Jeep, he told me there were no metalled roads, but that we would be taking the Numa Numa Trail which, in places, was 'a bit tricky on account of the rains'. In fact, before we reached our destination, we had repeatedly been up to the axles in mud and had forded the Laroma and Doybie rivers no fewer than twenty-three times.

Bougainville is a narrow island, about 130 miles in length, and is the largest of the Solomon group. At the time of my visit, which was after the Japanese had been driven out of their stronghold on Guadalcanal, it contained only a stubborn remnant of the enemy forces which had previously held it. The island bears the name of its discoverer, Louis Antoine de Bougainville, whose sailing ship *L'Etoile* put in here during his adventurous voyage round the world in 1766 to 1769. It is heavily forested and indescribably beautiful, with countless streams and high waterfalls cascading through the jungle down its steep mountains; two of which, Balbi and Bagana, are active volcanoes. Orchids and flowering vines, colourful birds and enormous, vividly-hued butterflies abound. The small Melanesian population, whose men were affectionately called the 'Fuzzy-wuzzies' by the Australian troops on account of their bushy hair, raises crops of coconut, bananas, taro, yams and sweet potatoes. A simple, friendly and deeply superstitious people, they regarded the War as something beyond their comprehension, a temporary visitation which, like a cyclone, would presently pass away and from which the only profit was the salvage of camp debris. Since the sixteenth century they had known many foreign overlords — the Spanish, the German, the British, the Australian, the Japanese and now the Australians again. From time to time we saw small groups of them, trudging impassively along the muddy trail, but willing to return our greetings with smiles revealing a flash of white teeth. The men wore coloured loin cloths and carried only a spear or a stick; the women invariably bore heavy burdens of kindling or foodstuffs.

'The men look lazy devils,' said my companion, who had stripped off his shirt as soon as we entered the humid forest. 'But they carried our wounded on their backs down to the dressing stations during the fighting.

'They just don't understand about the War,' he went on. 'You see them strolling around under gunfire as though they think they are bloody immortal. We tried to get them to wear tin hats, but their hair is like a doormat and the helmets just perched on top and they laughed themselves sick trying to make them stay on. They apparently think they are just as safe wearing a couple of bloody orchids in their hair — some kind of magic ju-ju, I reckon.' I had noticed that several of the men we passed had orchids tucked into their wiry mops; I like to believe they adorn themselves in this manner because they have an instinctive response to beauty, like many Polynesians and the highland tribes of New Guinea, whose adornment with flowers, shells and feathers is elaborate.

As we wound our way up the mountains into the cloud forest, the trees became taller and the strangling vines more dense. Here and there immense gums soared above the tree canopy, their narrow glaucous leaves contrasting with the darker hues below. Huge, luxuriant ferns and palms overhung the trail, every frond gleaming with pendant dewdrops which rained down on us as we brushed past. Long sprays of pink, yellow and white orchids and other epiphytes hung from the mossy trees. In the narrow gorges above the cascading streams there were occasional native bridges, incredibly flimsy constructions of liana vines and split bamboo, with one strand for the feet and one either side for the hands to grasp.

During the afternoon we came on the first signs of war, where shell-fire had stripped the trees of branches and the ground was littered with empty shell cases and the refuse of occupation by troops. A few miles further on there had evidently been protracted fighting and the forest was reduced to leafless and shattered tree stumps. The bullet-pocked skeleton of a Japanese Zero fighter plane stood grotesquely on its nose among the trees, reminding me that Japan's chief War Lord, Admiral Yamamoto, had been shot down while trying to land on Bougainville. We were now on the hog's-back of the Emperor Range. A sign nailed to a tree proudly announced, in the manner dear to all soldiers during the war: 'Kingsway Scenic Drive, opened 5 March '45 by Capt. J. A. King.' Later, as we breasted a very steep hill, another notice tersely commanded, 'Don't stop — don't change gear.' We engaged four-wheel drive and lurched up the zig-zag trail, spraying mud for ten feet on either side. The mountain battery we were seeking came into view as we reached the summit. It was well dug in and well camouflaged, overlooking the wide, jungle-clad valley beyond. Australian infantry occupied the steeply descending slopes and the enemy the blue hills beyond. The scene was peaceful and unmarred by gun fire.

I was cautiously greeted by the battery commander. A British officer was something of a curiosity in this theatre of war; but after explaining the details of my mission I was quickly made to feel welcome.

After inspecting the snub-nosed howitzers in their neatly sand-bagged emplacements, I sat on the edge of the escarpment with three of the officers and discussed their supply problems, which were numerous (*see* Plate 1). The main wave of hostilities had swung far west along the Pacific islands under the growing American naval victories. Pockets of Japanese resistance had been by-passed, leaving difficult mopping-up actions to be completed by Australian and American ground forces, of which this was one. But, as one of the officers put it: 'It's just as tough to winkle-out a couple of hundred Nips from this kind of cover as a thousand — and they never give up!' So, in this backwater of earlier large-scale hostilities, the war dragged on.

As the long evening shadows began to darken the valley, bottles of beer were produced and talk drifted away from technicalities. The officers were all in their twenties — a sheep farmer, a school gym instructor and a city-bred bank clerk. But they were all veterans in war, who had gained professional competence under fire. Like most Australians, they were physically tough, self-reliant and independently minded, with a casual conviction of superiority over both Yanks and Pommies when it came to jungle fighting. However, though I was probably the only British soldier they had ever met, they politely insisted that not all Pommies were as stuffy as they were made out to be. When later I mentioned that I had seen many of their compatriots during the Burmese and North African campaigns, in which I had been briefly involved, their reaction was one of envy. They had been deprived of any chance to take part in these wider spheres by the presence of the enemy in the off-shore Australasian islands. 'We are fighting a world war in our own back yard, stuck in this Godforsaken island,' said one.

That night, as I lay on my camp cot, enveloped in the musty odour of damp mosquito netting, I heard the far-distant rumble of heavy guns in the direction of the Bismarck Archipelago. I could see through the open end of my tent the bright sparkle of stars in the dark sky over the enemy-held hills. Crickets and cicadas were shrilling an endless chorus in the trees around my tent and when presently the guns ceased muttering, the sound was soporific in its constancy. I felt a foretaste of the peace which was daily drawing nearer, though I knew that in the valley below sentries were still peering alertly into the darkness and night patrols were probing the jungle. But the tide had turned irrevocably and the young Australians would soon return to their vast, sunlit country. Bougainville would heal its scars and again be an island paradise, remote from strife and ugliness.

Ever since that brief visit to Bougainville, the island remained in my memory as one of the places I most wanted to see again. There was something about its purity and isolation from the hurly-burly of the modern world which made it stand out from all the other Pacific islands which I had seen. Many had been irreparably scarred by the War, or, like the Hawaiian group, by the penalty of westernization. But Bougainville I felt, illogically perhaps, would retain both its beauty and its pristine innocence.

In 1972 the B.B.C. showed a television film which shattered my illusion so completely that even now I am sickened by its recollection. The film was concerned with the work of a mining company, which had been granted rights by the Australian Government to exploit the rich copper deposits in the mountains of Bougainville. In return for a derisory sum paid to the Melanesians, the engineers moved in with their giant excavators and proceeded to strip some thirty-seven square miles of virgin forest in order to enable them to extract more than

1. The author (*right*) on Bougainville Island during the Pacific campaign in 1945. With its rich, tropical forests and high waterfalls, it used to be the most beautiful of the Solomon islands, but has since been devastated by opencast copper mining. Below is a typical example of the irreparable scar left by this system of mineral exploitation.

2. Our explorations in the western Himalayas were difficult once the snow-line was crossed. Even at modest altitudes our jeeps frequently had to be man-handled. *Below*: A dugout canoe from a native village proved to be ideal for exploring the rivers which wind through the densely forested Chittagong Hill Tracts in Bangladesh.

200,000 tons of copper ore a year from the mountains. In a short space of time the island was swarming with imported labourers, equipment and buildings. Appalled and bewildered by the transformation of their homeland, the innocent Melanesians eventually protested when road-building threatened the sacred site of the resting places of their ancestors. The company then increased the rental for the land they had ruined. Modern open-cast mining, however carefully planned, causes unbelievable havoc over a huge area, not only where the extraction takes place, but also for the disposal of the tailings and the space needed for supporting installations and accommodation for the labour force. Rivers and the inshore waters are soon polluted. The gigantic scar which remains when the operation is completed can never be restored to look anything like the original site, no matter how much back-filling and re-planting is attempted. Moreover, although mining companies invariably promise restoration, the fact remains that no open-cast mine anywhere in the world has yet been completely restored.

The company responsible for the rape of Bougainville is internationally respected for its skills and for the contribution it makes to the economies of many countries. Some of its directors are public figures, intelligent people who are quickly distressed by accusations of lack of concern for the human environment. But their approach to the topic of conservation is sadly myopic. Like so many Europeans, Americans, Canadians and Japanese engaged in the exploitation of solid minerals, oil, or timber, they appear to fail to understand that conservation is not an emotional attitude and that it does not necessarily inhibit growth. They do not, it seems to me at the time of writing, understand that it implies diversity and the maintenance of the choice of options as essential ingredients to the quality of life. Neither the suave words of their public relations spokesmen, nor the soothing quality of their glossy annual reports to shareholders, can disguise the fact that their companies are in many instances damaging primitive communities in Australasia, Asia and South America. Bougainville will never be the same again. Its pristine aspect has gone for ever. In the name of progress its people have been irreparably harmed by an uninvited invasion from the modern world.

Obviously the western nations need essential minerals such as copper. Equally obviously a mining company's duty to its shareholders is to exploit such a resource as economically as possible. Open-cast mining is a quicker means of obtaining it than by old-fashioned tunnelling, which causes far less disturbance to the site. But when the ethical aspects of conservation become more widely recognized, the time will come when the interests and rights of the native communities concerned will be given much more serious consideration.

Twenty-seven years before exploitation struck Bougainville, the home-sick young Australian soldier had called it a God-forsaken island. Perhaps he had the gift of prophecy.

3 A Web of Survival

I saw my first Bindibu when I landed in an R.A.F. plane during the War to refuel in west-central Australia. The temporary airfield was a mere double row of markers in the middle of the stony desert, beside a few corrugated iron huts, a water tower and a lifeless wind-sock. From horizon to horizon not a single tree relieved the sun-scorched wilderness. The ground temperature was 110°F (44°C). While the plane was being re-fuelled I wandered over to the huts, mopping the perspiration which trickled down my face and soaked my shirt.

Turning the corner behind one of the huts, I found myself confronted by a Bindibu. He was squatting motionless in the shade, naked, coal black and expressionless. He did not look up as I appeared, but continued to gaze into the shimmering heat-haze. An untidy mop of black hair overhung his eyes; his leathery face was deeply furrowed, with a wispy, grizzled beard obscuring his chin. Around his lean waist was a single string, from which hung a flint knife. A veritable Stone Age man.

Following the line of his gaze, I could just make out the shapes of several stooped figures near the horizon. They were presumably his womenfolk, gathering the roots and beetle grubs which are the staple diet of the Bindibu. This amazing aboriginal people has inhabited the Australian desert for at least 10,000 years, surviving successfully in one of the most starkly hostile environments it is possible to imagine. Nowhere numerous, small family groups wander across the 1·3 million square miles of desert seeking food and following the rare rainfall, drinking from pools on all fours like animals. They are unbelievably skilled trackers and hunters, killing wallabies, emus, dingos, or lizards with throwing-sticks or stone-tipped spears. Like the Kalahari Bushmen, they escape the cold at night by erecting primitive windbreaks of spinifex grass, but have no ability in building or weaving. They do, however, plait vegetable fibres or use animal sinews for binding the heads of their stone axes. They have no permanent dwellings, no art and have never learned to raise crops or fashion even the simplest receptacle for storing food or water. Yet they survive and though regarded by most Australians as little better than scavenging animals, they have saved many a crashed air crew or lost prospector in the desolate outbacks where white men can die of dehydration in forty-eight hours.

Wherever there are deserts, man has contrived to settle in them permanently. Curiously, his adaptation to them has followed two very dissimilar paths. While the Australian Bindibus and the Kalahari Bushmen go stark naked, relying on their very dark pigmentation to repel the sun's rays, the Arabs and Berbers of the Sahara, the bedouin of Arabia and the nomads of the Great Indian Desert protect themselves by voluminous dark clothing which covers even their faces. A white man stranded in the desert can lose a quart of perspiration in an hour and his body weight declines very rapidly. Sunburn accelerates the onset of delirium and even if he has ample water he is unlikely to survive for more than a few days unless he can find shade. On the other hand, a camel without water can lose 22% of its body weight during a week-long desert crossing, but is quickly restored by drinking.

Having seen only seven of the twelve great deserts of the world, I have only a slight knowledge of the many life forms which inhabit them. Nevertheless, and in spite of the all too apparent negative aspects associated with them, I have always been fascinated by the complex manner in which humans, wildlife and vegetation adapt themselves to the harsh conditions of a desert environment.

Apart from a brief spell in the relatively benign Mojave Desert of California, which I saw in the full glory of its flowering, I did not see a real desert until 1942, when I drove from

Egypt across Libya in the wake of the Eighth Army. My first surprise was to find that after the gruelling heat of the day, the temperature dropped by forty-eight degrees at night. The low humidity in deserts allows the daytime heat to be reduced with extreme rapidity; without this drastic reduction no animal or plant life could survive.

On this first desert crossing I was able to see very little wildlife because of the billowing dust and noise of the military convoys. However, when I stopped my jeep to replenish the radiator, a desert lark dropped from the cloudless sky to seek shade beneath the vehicle and to drink eagerly the drops of water trickling from the radiator overflow. Such opportunism and quick adaptation to anything contributing to survival is typical of desert creatures.

This incident reminded me that when I had stopped at an isolated filling station in the Mojave, a swarm of house sparrows sheltering in the trees had descended immediately to pick the barbecued butterflies and grasshoppers from the hot radiator grille of my car. The pump attendant told me that the sparrows 'had been doing it for years'.

The Libyan Desert, which from the ground looks so featureless, presented a very different aspect when later I flew over it at dawn. As soon as one left the coastal area, which was heavily scarred by the passage of tanks and pockmarked by thousands of shell craters, the real face of the desert was revealed. From an altitude of 10,000 feet, in the clear side-light of the rising sun, every coalescent dune and undulation cast a strong shadow, forming a lace-like pattern of great beauty. The direction of the prevailing wind could be seen by the long slopes on the windward side and the sharp descent on the leeward side of the dunes. Farther south the ground was more level, broken here and there only by patches of crescentic barchan dunes.

A month later, when the victorious Eighth Army had linked hands with the First in Tunisia, I was able to fly along the northern parts of the Sahara, which are dotted with oases. From a high-flying aircraft they looked like large bomb craters half filled with green water. Closer inspection showed the green to be clusters of date palms sheltering villages. The edges of the craters were high dunes of wind-borne sand piled against log barricades, each with a diameter of about 500 yards. Some of these circular man-made dunes were 100 feet high, yet still the invading sand was burying the trees and silting into the wells. Linking each oasis to its neighbour was a winding camel track, looking from the air like the minute trail of a beetle across the sand. Oases are, of course, of vital importance to trans-Saharan migrant birds. On one occasion when I was staying in an oasis in Morocco during the migratory season, the entire bird population appeared to change every day, one morning every bush and tree swarming with small warblers and the next with chats and blackbirds.

It was not until 1963 that I had an opportunity to compare the Australian and African deserts with the Arabian. I had been invited to investigate the problems facing the rapidly disappearing wildlife of Jordan and to help the government to devise a programme of conservation. The task was complex, but with the aid of a team of distinguished specialists, our explorations were completed in eight weeks. Among my colleagues were expert ecologists such as Sir Julian Huxley, Max Nicholson and Duncan Poore. Travelling in Land-Rovers and seldom using Jordan's few highways, we covered about 3,000 miles, from the Sea of Galilee down the whole length of the Great Rift to the Wadi Rum and Aqaba and far out into the northern and southern parts of the desert. Apart from having to leave two wrecked vehicles in the desert, it was a wholly delightful experience. As an outcome of our labours, the Azraq Desert National Park was created and the now flourishing Royal Jordanian Society for the Conservation of Nature was formed.

During our explorations we enjoyed the hospitality of many bedouin camps. Even on the briefest visit we were invariably received with great courtesy and invited to drink *liban*, made from curdled sheep's milk and drunk from a communal tin bowl. On other occasions we attended ceremonial *mansef* feasts in the great black goat-hair tents of important sheikhs. A *mansef* is a highly ritualized affair, with guests sitting cross-legged on colourful tribal carpets, or reclining against decorative camel saddles, in strict order of precedence either side of the host. Speeches of welcome, compliments and presents are exchanged with great dignity and with lengthy pauses to enable their significance to be fully savoured, the passage of time having little importance to the bedouin. Coffee spiced with cardamom is then served from a long-spouted brass pot into minute cups, the first of which is presented to the chief guest of honour. Protocol requires that the thick, sweet liquid should be sipped slowly, with appropriate expressions of rapture. On the third round the tiny cup is rocked from side to side to denote polite refusal. Finally two men stagger in with the *pièce de résistance*, a mound of saffron-dyed rice on an iron platter, surmounted by the carcasses of several broiled sheep, whose glassy eyes, yellow teeth and bristling chins are inclined to unnerve the neophyte. Amid applause, the dish is landed at the guest of honour's feet and all gather round. Scalding fat is poured over the edifice and the carcasses are dismembered by hand, each guest scooping handfuls of hot rice at intervals. Food may be touched only with the right hand, the left being 'unclean'. Extreme skill is involved in kneading the rice into golf-ball-size bullets, which are flicked by the thumb into the mouth; if too much fat has been squeezed from the rice, the ball disintegrates in mid flight. When only skeletons remain, the sheikh throws them to his expectant hounds. With much polite and resonant belching and slapping of stomachs, the guests then cleanse their hands with sand and sprinkle them with rose-water before relaxing again against the camel saddles. Tiny glasses of mint tea are sipped while listening to a philosophical monologue by the sheikh. The bedouin are accomplished talkers with a rich sense of humour, weaving their stories with complex analogies and drawing freely on tribal histories or the Koran to illustrate their points.

Unfortunately they are also adept in construing the sometimes conflicting edicts of the Koran to suit their passionate devotion to the chase. While admitting that it forbids cruelty to animals, they are quick to point out that it also extols the manly virtues of hunting. Jordan was once teeming with game, as can be seen from the beautiful murals in the many ruins of the eighth-century hunting lodges of the Umayyad caliphs scattered throughout the desert, in areas which were then forested. The present century has seen the last of the addax antelope, the roe and fallow deer, the wild ass, the Syrian bear, the cheetah, the crocodile and the Arabian ostrich. A very small number of Arabian oryx still survive in the southern part of the Arabian peninsula, but even the once extremely numerous gazelles are nearing extinction. Jordan represents one of the saddest examples of a partly man-made desert, in which nearly all the larger animals have been ruthlessly destroyed. The desert has been progressively enlarged by the felling of forests for fuel and by persistent over-grazing by unlimited numbers of ravenous goats and camels. For lack of trees, the bedouin women now pull up the desert shrubs, denuding another quarter of an acre of desert every time they boil a pot of coffee.

Not a single river relieves the desperate shortage of water in the Arabian desert. The River Jordan, which divides Israel from the Hashemite Kingdom of Jordan, contributes nothing; the long range of mountains through which it flows spills its few streams westward and gives only Israel the benefit of its rain shadow. One third of the Arabian desert is sand, the remainder being what the bedouin call *hamada*, a hard flinty waste dotted with brittle shrublets which survive by thrusting their grotesquely long roots deep into the ground near the usually bone-dry *wadis*. Far to the south in the Empty Quarter the sand is deep and piled up by the hot wind into the world's highest dunes, some 700 feet high. To the north-east the valleys of the Tigris and Euphrates form what was once called the 'Fertile Crescent', where prehistoric man first learned to raise crops and to bring wild cattle under domestication. Unhappily, by doing so, and by measuring his wealth by the number of cattle he owned, he created a way of life which, carried to extremes in many torrid lands throughout the world, has converted once fertile grazing into vast and total deserts.

Our work in Jordan enabled us to study the inter-relationships of desert organisms and their elaborate adaptations to excessive aridity and heat, in which reproduction is governed by the rare and irregular rainfall. From the bedouin down to the lowliest plant or arthropod, the pattern of adaptability was apparent. The lives of the nomadic bedouin are ruled by their ceaseless search for grazing and water, for which they have fought many a bloody battle. Diurnal birds appear to be at a particular disadvantage because of their narrow tolerance of extreme heat and rapid bodily metabolism, yet by a variety of means they succeed, obtaining the water they need from their food and escaping the worst of the heat by feeding at dawn and dusk. When the erratic conditions are favourable to breeding, they come into sexual condition to do so far more rapidly than birds in temperate regions, and when conditions are unfavourable they make no attempt to breed. Instead of brooding their eggs, many desert species such as the coursers, which lay their eggs on bare stony ground, stand with half-open wings to shield them from the excessive heat of the sun.

Sandgrouse, which are very dependent on water, fly great distances every day to waterholes; when nesting, they soak their belly feathers in water before flying back to their nests, so that their chicks can benefit from the moisture. Normal feathers would quickly shed the water, but the belly feathers of sandgrouse have downy end-tufts which draw up the moisture by capillary attraction and retain it by means of uniquely interwoven barbels. The numerous species of desert larks show a wide range of physiological developments to suit specialized feeding behaviour, ranging from the long curved bill of the hoopoe lark, which digs and probes for food, to the grotesquely massive bill and bulging jaw muscles of the thick-billed lark, which feeds on the extremely hard kernels of certain desert plants.

Among the desert rodents even more specialized developments can be seen. Many of them pass their entire brief lives without drinking. They urinate seldom and lose very little moisture in their solid excretions. Feeding on dry seeds, their intake of moisture is also very limited. When the rat-like gerbils return to their burrows after a night's foraging, they seal the entrances to exclude the heat and to retain humidity, their snug dormitories thus remaining thirty degrees cooler than outside, while their breath raises the humidity. In periods of extreme heat they go into a state of estivation, when their bodily metabolism slows down and their temperature decreases. Even more extreme is the behaviour of the desert hare, which practises a form of rumination and refection, not as in typical large ruminant mammals by regurgitation, but by taking its droppings direct from the anus and swallowing them again without chewing, in order to retain the moisture.

To detect the approach of enemies, many desert animals have developed huge external ears and enlarged resonance chambers in their skulls. The jumping jerboas have powerful hind legs and hairy toes to enable them to obtain purchase in soft sand and long tails enabling them to change direction in mid air while jumping. The reptiles also exhibit specialization. Some of the lizards and geckos have fringed toes to help them to move more quickly in soft sand, while others have valved nostrils enabling them to dive instantly into the sand and to travel long distances beneath it. Perhaps the most dramatic survival mechanism is seen in the freshwater shrimps which live in desert pools. When pools which have been dry for years are suddenly filled by a desert storm, thousands of these little arthropods, which have lain dormant as eggs in the sun-baked mud, hatch out and reproduce themselves by the same strangely fortuitous cycle. There is an authentic record of one such example of a Californian shrimp which hatched successfully after the eggs had lain for twenty-five years in the cement-hard ground of the desert.

Deserts were classified by a mathematical formula combining temperature and rainfall by an Austrian scientist named Wladimir Koppen. Pure deserts, by his formula, have high temperatures and less than ten inches of rainfall per annum. These represent 14% of all land on Earth. Another 14% is represented by semi-arid steppes, with high annual temperatures and between ten and twenty inches of rain. Thus one square mile in every seven of Earth's fifty-six million square miles is composed of desert or semi-desert. At present these are unproductive of foodstuffs for the world's exploding human population. I find some comfort in the belief that modern technology is capable of making them productive. Experiments in the Sahara, the world's largest desert, have shown that splendid crops can be raised by boring for water. In Iraq, a big increase in agricultural output was achieved by a vigorous campaign of well-boring. Such small-scale work is encouraging, but it is unlikely that the water table beneath most deserts is high enough to last for very long. The ultimate solution will undoubtedly lie in irrigation from the nuclear-powered distillation of sea water. With one third of the world's human population already living at near starvation level, the cultivation of these immense reserves of land cannot be postponed much longer. We have been willing to spend gigantic sums of money on the extraction of oil, copper, borax, salt, potash and gypsum from deserts, chiefly for the benefit of the rich democracies. The cost of cultivating the deserts would also be colossal, though probably less than has already willingly been spent by the United States and the USSR on the exploration of outer space. It is simply a question of getting our priorities right. But if deserts are to be used for the benefit of man, we must also recognize their value both to science and to wildlife and set aside ample areas where the intricate natural ecology of desert life can continue unmolested.

The Latin derivation of the word desert means 'abandoned'. Deserts have not been abandoned by nature. Far from accepting this definition, we should regard deserts as biological capital and as one of the last unruptured strands in the now tattered web of human survival.

4 The Problem People

'Take the Otavalo Indians,' said my Ecuadorian friend. 'They are industrious and have plenty of commercial sense. They put their native crafts such as weaving, pottery and raising vegetables, to profitable use. Many of them are getting rich since the tourists began arriving in bus-loads at their market. Pretty soon you'll see them using automobiles instead of donkeys. In fact, they are becoming integrated into modern society and are contributing to the economy. But the Colorados,' he frowned and shook his head, 'they are a problem. They just don't want to be integrated — and they're as lazy as hell.'

We were walking in single file along a muddy trail through the rich jungle which crowds closely around the valleys below Quito, Ecuador's capital city in the clouds. It was steaming hot under the trees, but we had not far to go. A single slippery log laid across a racing stream took us to the domain of the Colorados. The trees were less dense now and in the patches of sunlight enormous *Morpho* butterflies glided on kingfisher-blue wings with a span of five inches. Iridescent green humming-birds darted and hovered among the red vine flowers.

Presently we passed plantations of bananas. They were neither well kept nor symmetrical, but the fat green fruit was hanging in abundance above the invading cup-of-gold vines and white datura lilies. Dancing blizzards of violet and green *Prepona* and scarlet and yellow *Heliconius* butterflies had been tempted down from the sunlit tree-tops to feast on the juices of the fallen fruit. This was Ecuador at its most glamorous. They say that if you toss a seed over your shoulder in Ecuador you step back into a tree. Growing fruit or crops in the deep, rich soil of the valleys is no problem — the only difficulty is getting it to market. Weeding is something only the rich can afford. And when nature provides such a bounty of native fruits, who needs an aching back anyway?

At the summit of a small hill we came to a clearing surrounded by coconut palms and bamboo huts thatched with banana leaves — the village of the Colorados. A group of men, women and children were squatting in the shade of a huge breadfruit tree. The men were much taller and of finer physique than the Otavalos. Their coffee-coloured bodies and limbs were horizontally striped with a blue-black dye and their only garments black and white horizontally striped loin cloths. Their hair was heavily plastered into a stiff peak over their foreheads and was of a brilliant orange colour, giving the impression of wearing orange cloth caps. This unusual effect is obtained by grinding the oily seeds of the *Bixa orellana* tree and plastering the resultant paste on the hair, which then dries in the required cap-shape to the hardness of wood. The chief was distinguished by a colourful shawl and broad silver bangles. The women were squat and rather unbecoming, wearing only knee-length skirts, horizontally striped in many colours. Their glossy black hair hung to their waists (*see* Plate 3). Around their necks were green or white bead necklaces. One young woman, though dressed like the others, was startlingly blonde, fair-skinned and tall; her features were distinctly European and I wondered how she had come to marry a Colorado Indian living in the midst of the jungle. Two coffee-coloured children clung to her skirt and watched us curiously while my friend chatted to the chief. By comparison with the very gay Kuna Indians of the Las Perlas Islands, off Panama, whom I had just visited, the little jungle community was unsmiling and sombre. According to my companion, both men and women of the Colorados, like many of the Peruvian hill tribes, live permanently under the influence of opiates or alcohol.

We were shown over the village. There was not much to see. The huts were constructed with little skill and looked incapable of withstanding the heavy rain of the region. The only sign of modernity was some rusting corrugated iron roofing on one of the huts. Behind one of these we came on an emaciated old woman lying on the ground. She looked ill and was covered with flies. My friend explained that she was waiting for the local witch doctor.

'You see that pit,' he said, pointing to a square hole in the ground. 'The witch doctor will put her in there for the night and will burn some aromatic herbs around her while he recites his mumbo-jumbo. It's all the same to him whether she has a fever, cancer, or an outbreak of boils — the only difference will be the price he charges her relatives. If she gets well he will be applauded. If she doesn't, nobody is going to bother much anyway. He can't lose. He's the only rich man in the tribe and they say he lives in a fine house up on the highway. A cunning old devil.'

I looked at the old woman, whose eyes were her only sign of life. 'Shouldn't you get her to hospital?' I asked.

'She wouldn't go,' he replied, with a shrug. 'Besides, the hospital is full of townfolk and nobody is going to worry about a Colorado dying of old age. There are so few of them left that they are terribly in-bred and are going to die out anyway before long.'

Ecuador, like most South American countries, has numerous 'problem' tribes such as the Colorados — primitive people who managed to survive the Spanish conquest, but are unable to meet the far more radical challenge of the twentieth century. Many such remnant tribes inhabit the foothills of the Andes and the still vast jungles in the lowlands. Some are undoubtedly so fiercely resistant to the modern world that they do not hesitate to kill strangers in their territories. Head-hunting and head-shrinking are still practised by them, though most of the shrunken heads offered to tourists in the cities are not human but monkey-heads. From time to time parties of surveyors or engineers disappear in the jungle and the military are then sent on punitive expeditions to burn down a few villages. But though they not infrequently find the heads of the lost surveyors or engineers on stakes, or hanging from the roof of a hut, it is almost impossible to find and punish the culprits. A

shoot-on-sight policy is therefore adopted until a sufficient toll
has been taken to satisfy the law.

To understand what befell the civilizations of the Americas,
one must go back three thousand years to the ancient Sun
Kingdoms of the Aztecs of Mexico, the Mayas of the jungles of
Guatemala, Yucatán and British Honduras and the Incas of
western South America. Ali three of these once powerful civilizations were destroyed in their turn by the Spanish invaders
during the sixteenth to eighteenth centuries. They were literally exterminated and their extremely rich cultures all but
obliterated, with a thoroughness which has few parallels in
history. But for the enveloping jungle, which quickly hid the
remains of the Maya buildings, and but for the enormity of the
task of destroying the gigantic Aztec and Inca monuments and
fortress cities, nothing would have survived. Cortés and his
conquistadores landed in 1519. By 1525 he had wiped out the
Aztecs. By 1697 Martin de Ursua had completed the task begun by Cortés and had exterminated the Maya civilization. In
a single half-hour's slaughter in 1781 Francisco Pizarro
massacred the last 6,000 unarmed Incas, whom he had invited
to pay him a social visit at the township of Cajamarca. Thus
terminated one of the bloodiest and most barbarous periods
ever to blacken the annals of Christian conquest. Though every
action was taken under the guise of introducing Christianity
into a pagan region (and it is said that Pizarro's priests preached
a sermon to the puzzled Incas at Cajamarca before signalling
the hidden cannon and arquebuses to open fire on the congre-
gation) the primary object was to secure the almost unbelievable quantities of gold treasures of the Sun Kingdoms.

Although by today's standards the Aztecs, Mayas and Incas
were obviously savages, who practised human sacrifice on a
gigantic scale to propitiate their gods, they were extremely industrious, with unique skills in building, mining, pottery,
weaving and above all in gold ornamentation. Their passion for
the use of gold and the magnificence of their artistry in its
application has rarely, if ever, been surpassed.

There is no knowing how many boatloads of gold and silver
treasure were taken to Spain during the Spanish conquest.

Extremely few relics survived. Everything was melted down into ingots at the foundries of Toledo, Sevilla, or Segovia, to pay for Spain's interminable European wars. Spanish historians did, however, leave a graphic documentation of some of the looted treasure. An eye-witness account survives of the first sight of the gold-plated city of Cuzco. Rebuilt in AD 1400, Cuzco still stands, perched at 11,000 feet above sea level in the Andes mountains. It provides a striking example not only of the expertise of the Incas in city planning, but of their extraordinary skill as stone masons. Without a trace of mortar, every stone in the still perfectly aligned walls and terraces fits so perfectly that one would think it had been cut and polished by machine, though the Incas used only flint tools and rock abrasives to obtain this marvellous precision. Here, and at the neighbouring fortress city of Pisac, which contains the giant sundial called 'the hitching-place of the sun', one can see the perfection of the typical Inca trapezoidal gateways and windows, which have stood undistorted for nearly six hundred years.

When first seen by the Spanish, Cuzco, like all the principal Inca centres, was a lavishly gold-plated city. In the centre stood the *Curi-cancha* — the Golden Enclosure and the Temple of the Sun, massively covered with gold plating. There were five golden fountains, numerous life-size gold statues, a garden planted with solid gold flowers, a cornfield of real golden corn and a herd of gold llamas guarded by gold statues of shepherds. Even the thatching of the surrounding buildings gleamed with golden straws which had been woven into the thatch. No wonder the chronicler wrote that he could scarcely believe his eyes. But he expressed no contrition that every scrap of this fantastic treasure was speedily looted by his compatriots.

Another carefully documented account tells of the ransom paid by the Lord-Inca Atahualpa, for his release by the Spanish. The price demanded was as much gold treasure as would fill a room 25 feet by 15 and higher than a tall man could stretch his arm. Incredible though it may seem, the golden hoard was duly delivered. The simple Atahualpa was then put to death by his laughing captors.

3. A family of forest-dwelling Colorado Indians of Ecuador. Like many other South American tribes, they seem doomed to early extinction. The men plaster their hair with an orange paste made from the seeds of the *Bixa orellana* tree. *Below*: Machu Picchu, the lost city of the Incas, which was hidden by the jungle for 400 years until rediscovered by Hiram Bingham.

4. The remote lowland terai of western Nepal gave me an opportunity to camp where tigers were still relatively unmolested. During the night a curious tigress inspected us, coming within 24 feet of my tent. This beautiful area is now the Sukla Phanta Wildlife Reserve. *Below*: The two-day journey from India involved some difficult river crossings.

Cuzco was only one of a chain of high fortress cities built by the Incas along their 2,000-mile highway between Quito in Ecuador and Lake Titikaka, which lies between Peru and Bolivia. I have had the pleasure of visiting several of them during my travels. By far the most spectacular is Machu Picchu, which since its re-discovery by Hiram Bingham after it had stood enveloped by the jungle for four hundred years, has become a romantic attraction to tourists hardy enough to make the journey into the mountains.

When I first saw it, soaring above its countless terraces, which rise tier upon tier above the billowing clouds of the Urubamba River gorge, I felt transported back to the mystical fairyland castles of my early childhood, to the stories of Hans Andersen and Grimm (*see* Plate 3). It is almost beyond belief that so many thousands of tons of huge, perfectly fashioned rocks could have been hewn and carried up such stupendous and in places almost vertical slopes. Yet there the fortress city stands, complete with its intricate, narrow streets, terraces, store-houses, aqueducts, lookout posts and once gold-plated stone throne of the Lord-Inca. But, as a naturalist, I found the long journey to Machu Picchu almost as rewarding as the destination. As I entered the long gorge of the Urubamba I saw my first Andean condors, sailing effortlessly above the high peaks on wings with a spread of nearly eleven feet. In the racing white water of the river, several pairs of the rare Peruvian torrent ducks showed themselves, swimming powerfully among the whirlpools, or bobbing like corks at the foot of a thundering waterfall. While I toiled up the final rough trail to the cloud city, supercilious llamas and their woolly, Walt Disneyesque young accompanied me, fluttering their glamorously long eye-lashes at me; when I was tempted to snap a close-up portrait of one, it showed a sensitive disapproval by spitting with devastating accuracy into the lens. Such incidents enrich one's travels. But I am digressing.

If Ecuador, Colombia and Peru are today embarrassed by the problem of their surviving primitive tribes, Brazil has been frankly determined that its Indians should not be allowed to stand in the way of progress. The Spanish and Portuguese conquests in South America set a pattern of ruthless extermination which was all too easy to imitate. The Spaniards slaughtered in the name of Christianity, the Portuguese, who controlled the Amazon basin, were perhaps less ruthless, though equally determined on plunder to fill their coffers. By the time independence from foreign oppression was achieved, millions had died. Most of the remaining tribes had either accepted integration, like the Otavalos of Ecuador, or had been forced to take refuge in the inhospitable highlands of the Andes, or in the vast forests of the Amazon.

Only from an aircraft can one gain any real impression of the gigantic and impenetrable nature of the Amazon forests, which extend like a green, arboreal ocean of tens of thousands of square miles. Through this rich jungle wind the innumerable tributaries of the world's greatest river — the Amazon, which has a length of 3,900 miles and drains an area almost as large as the United States. Apart from an occasional slender canoe on the twisting waterways, one sees no sign of the 60,000 to 80,000 Indians of various tribes who live in the forests. There is something vaguely menacing about the sheer size and uniformity of the endless green panorama of trees which stretches from horizon to horizon below a high-flying aircraft. Several pilots have told me that they dislike flying over it, because it offers no chance whatever of survival in the event of a forced landing. Strangely enough, I had reason to understand their attitude when, on my first flight across Brazil in a war-time bomber of the Royal Canadian Air Force, one of the four engines developed an oil leak and seized up. Although I knew that the plane could fly perfectly safely on three engines, I was extremely relieved when two hours later we landed at Belém.

Having once seen the size and nature of the Amazon forests, it is not difficult to understand why some of the Indian tribes which inhabit this unmapped wilderness have never seen a white man. So long as access was limited to the rivers, any stranger who attempted to penetrate the area was easily killed with poisoned arrows shot from the safety of the enveloping jungle. Very few of those who made such an attempt were ever heard of again. The disappearance of Colonel Percy Fawcett

in 1925 during his expedition to the Mato Grosso to locate the
mythical 'lost city' of the Xingú Indians, was only one of a long
series of similar incidents involving explorers, prospectors,
missionaries and government officials. Driven into their last
stronghold, the Indians were determined to defend it. The hard
core of resistance were the tribes of the Xingú, whose territories
lie beyond the aptly named Rio das Mortes — the River of
Deaths. Their success was an obvious reproach to the Brazilian
Government.

The coming of independence to Brazil did not, of course,
halt the harassment of the Indians — it was merely continued
less openly. In recent times the simple Indians were impressed
to learn that a special government body — the Indian Protection Service — had been created to look after their interests.
Before long, however, ugly rumours began circulating that the
new government agency had a far from paternalistic interest in
its charges. An enquiry was held and in 1967 the Ministry of
the Interior published its findings. These showed that the
Director of the Indian Protection Service and some hundreds
of its officials had for years deliberately encouraged the killing
and torture of Indians. In order to facilitate the expropriation
of tribal lands for the benefit of speculators, several thousand
Indians had been systematically inoculated with smallpox and
a number of villages had been dynamited by the Protection
Service. An independent report published by a reputable
French magazine also mentioned the distribution by helicopter
of cholera-infected clothing in some jungle villages. It is difficult to understand why the disclosures in the Brazilian Government report, which in substance resembled Hitler's 'final
solution' for the Jews and Stalin's extermination of the Kulaks,
aroused so little attention in the world's press. Perhaps it was
because the illiterate 'problem people' of South America had
no spokesman in the world's councils. Like the Red Indians of
North America and the aborigines of Australia, they were,
after all, to the average man, mere savages.

Today Brazil is following the solution adopted for the surviving North American Indians, by the creation of reserves,
such as the Parque Nacional do Xingú, into which those tribes

which do not accept integration into modern society will be gradually driven. A new northern reserve, in the Serra Tumucumaque, which adjoins the frontier with Surinam, will be far larger than any yet created by other countries as tribal reservations. How long its forests or minerals will remain unexploited by the white man remains to be seen. Already major parts of the Xingú and Aripuanan sanctuaries have been expropriated. Of the 230 Indian tribes listed in 1900, only fifty-two now survive and the Minister of the Interior has issued a clear warning: 'Their preservation in reserves is interesting but academic — they must be integrated into our society as quickly as possible.' Meanwhile, the Mato Grosso and the tribes of the Xingú are doomed by the construction of a 1,200-mile highway through the once impregnable forests of central Brazil. This grandiose project, involving the clearance of a strip 12 miles wide for settlement the full length of the Transamazonian and Cuiabá-Santarém highways, represents the destruction of 50,000 square miles of virgin forest. In spite of a warning by the Instituto Brasileiro de Geográfica that 'a disaster of enormous proportions is imminent', the work is proceeding at break-neck pace. On this occasion, however, the Brazilian Government, aware of the impending ecological disaster, had the foresight to invite international co-operation in studying the region ahead of the progress of the highway. The Royal Society and the National Geographical Society of Britain were quick to respond to this unique opportunity. A total of forty-four British and twenty Brazilian scientists carried out detailed studies of the geography, soil, botany, zoology, medical problems and tribal customs of the region. The magnificently illustrated account of the work of this joint expedition, by the explorer-naturalist Anthony Smith in his book *Mato Grosso*, is a fascinating and sensitively written story. If only the means existed for obliging politicians and land speculators to read it, many of the eco-catastrophes which are inflicted on wilderness areas could so easily be reduced.

Considered objectively, the fate of the South American Indians is in no way very different from that which has befallen primitive peoples in other continents. It is merely happening a

little later. The tribes are individually brave and skilful, but
have never even approached coalescence into nationhood. No
one tribe is sufficiently numerous to achieve leadership and
they remain isolated by their 1,700 different languages. Realists
will point out that one of the most frequent causes for the
extinction of a species is an inability to withstand competition,
or to adapt to a changing environment. In this respect the
remaining primitive races of *Homo sapiens* might be regarded
as having reached the end of their evolutionary tethers. But
primitive life forms are capable of persisting, if left undisturbed, for a very long time, as can be seen in the defenceless
marsupials of Australia, which have survived in that continent
in an astonishing variety of species simply because of the
absence of large carnivores among the native fauna. There is
no evidence to suggest that the millions of Indians who inhabited North and South America before the coming of the
predatory white man were on the point of dying out by natural
evolution. They were defeated because they lacked cohesion
and modern weapons with which to defend themselves. The
North American Indians could not withstand the Winchester
repeating rifle. The South American tribes are losing the
natural protection of the forests of the Amazon basin because
they cannot resist the bulldozer, the helicopter and the aero-
plane. Once airstrips and roads appear, they simply give in,
or withdraw further into the jungle. Though no longer persecuted with the ruthlessness of the Spaniards or the Indian
Protection Service, they live under the unspoken edict

> '. . . thou shalt not kill; but need'st not strive
> officiously to stay alive.'

The history of the disposal of 'the Indian problem' in North
America during the nineteenth century is, of course, much
better known than that of the South. It can be said to have
begun with the admirable North West Territory Ordinance of
1787. How well this reads today! 'The utmost good faith shall
always be observed towards the Indians. Their lands and
property shall never be taken from them without their consent.'

Yet only forty-three years later the Indian Removal Act was passed, permitting coercion to be used. Within the next ten years 100,000 Indians had been driven westward to make way for white settlers. Writing in 1831, the Comte de Tocqueville noted that 'whilst the savages were endeavouring to civilize themselves, the Europeans continued to surround them on every side and to confine them within narrower limits. The Indians have been ruined by a competition which they have not the means of resisting. They were isolated . . . a little colony of troublesome strangers in the midst of a numerous and dominant people.'

The California gold rush accelerated the process, as thousands of white families migrated westward. The Indians resisted and for thirty years there was open warfare, with terrible massacres on both sides, but with victory always certain for the well-armed and well-disciplined United States Army. Attempts to settle the Indians in restricted tribal territories failed because these were not large enough, nor safe from white encroachment. The millions of bison on which they depended for food and winter clothing were deliberately exterminated in the Great Plains, in order that the white man could travel without fear of attack by Indians. The General Allotment Act of 1887, which attempted to placate the tribes by the provision of rations and annual payments, was bitterly opposed by the anti-Indian elements in Congress, who maintained that it only made the Indians more difficult to assimilate into the American way of life. From the middle of the nineteenth century the Indian population began a steep decline, which was accelerated by epidemics of cholera and smallpox. A comfortable impression was gained that they were dying out so fast that they would soon vanish altogether; therefore there was no need to seek their views about their future. By 1920, however, it was realized that the Indian population was again rising and that an investigation of their plight was necessary. A survey was completed by 1926. This showed that the tribes had become very dispirited. They had no educational facilities and were totally unadjusted to the modern world by which they were surrounded. The Indian Reorganization Act of 1934 made belated though strenuous efforts to make amends. Indians were no longer treated as prisoners in the reservations and were given increasing powers of self-government. Although since then they have been treated with reasonable humanity and have even enjoyed the privilege of successfully suing the United States Government for payment for expropriated tribal land, they remain a stubbornly insoluble social problem. Within the reserves, they are wards of the State. Outside them, they forfeit their rights to education and welfare benefits. Bitter memories of the wrongs done to their forebears are not removed by the earnest efforts now being made to educate them. The rebellion at Wounded Knee in South Dakota in 1973, at the site of the massacre of more than 200 Sioux men, women and children by the United States cavalry in 1890, was symptomatic of this deep-rooted resentment.

In the course of my travels, I have seen some of the Indian reservations in North America, ranging from that of the Navahos of New Mexico to the Ojibwas of southern Canada. Although they are obviously places of enjoyment to the thousands of tourists who visit them, I found them inescapably depressing. The listless expressions on the faces of the men who dutifully repeat the now meaningless ritual dances, for the benefit of the photographers, still haunt me. The beautiful bead-work, feather ornaments and pottery which are now being produced in profusion as a source of income for the reservations, have lost all trace of their original tribal significance and are made without love or satisfaction. The young Indians in their blue jeans and Stetson hats who drift into the amusement arcades of the towns are confused and resentful, knowing themselves to belong neither to the tribal world of the past, nor to the materialistic world of the present. It is too much to expect that the conscientious efforts of the young white sociologists, who are trying to fit them into the twentieth-century pattern of life, while at the same time encouraging the retention of tribal customs and crafts in the reservations, can succeed.

In North America, the Eskimos alone have escaped the fate which has overtaken all the other primitive peoples of the continent. There was little to tempt the white man to exploit their icy domains; by the time modern technology provided relatively easy access to the Canadian Arctic, the age of ruthless exploitation was past. With great wisdom, the Canadian Government is protecting the Eskimos and their rich cultural heritage from the abuses suffered by the tribes of the United States and South America. Some of the primitive tribes of Africa and the New Guinea highlands have also been given extensive and wisely administered sanctuary lands.

I once accompanied, as naturalist-lecturer, a small group of well-behaved tourists, who made an unscheduled landing by rubber dinghy at an extremely remote village of stilted bamboo huts in a mangrove swamp on the West Irian coast of New Guinea. The very primitive Asmat tribes of the region were, and occasionally still are, head-hunters (*see* Plate 11). About fifty shouting, coal-black men, some completely naked, rushed into the water to meet us. They wore white cockatoo feather head-dresses mounted on cuscus-skin caps. Their bodies and limbs were boldly striped with white and through the septums of their noses they wore large circular ornaments made from nautilus shells. All were armed with feathered spears or bows and arrows. As we approached, they threw handfuls of lime at us, as an indication of friendly greeting.

Through an Indonesian interpreter we learned that we were the first white people they had seen since some Australian escaped prisoners of war had taken refuge there from the Japanese in 1944. During our stay of more than an hour, every man, woman and child in the village, except the nubile girls, who were kept hidden, danced around us in the liquid mud, chanting and ululating with great enthusiasm. We learned that they lived on a diet of fish, sago and jungle fruits. They planted no crops, but everything they possessed showed their virile artistic genius in carving, or decoration with shells or feathers. The blades of their spears and long daggers were made from the shin-bones of cassowaries. Worshipping their ancestors who were depicted on their magnificently carved *bis* poles and on the prows of their long, eight-man dugout war canoes, they lived in a lurid world of spirits and taboos. Every decision, even the selection of the next sago palm to be felled for the extraction of its starchy pith, was subject to elaborate ritual ceremonies and rhythmic dancing. They had access to no modern medicines and their expectation of life was short; but they lived in perfect equilibrium with their natural environment, destroying nothing wilfully and taking from the sea or forest only what was needed for survival or adornment.

Looking back later on this fascinating glimpse of a lost world, I could not escape a feeling of unease and of intrusion. Though the people I had accompanied had behaved with exemplary good manners, we represented the thin edge of the tourist wedge. Sooner or later others would follow and the innocent little community would change under their influence. These were almost literally Stone Age people. Even to see one smoking a modern cigarette, awkwardly held between thumb and finger, was to see the beginning of the end. I wished we had not landed; such unique relics of man's early history should remain completely undisturbed. The Indonesian Government's well-meaning campaign to suppress the Asmat *bis* poles and long-houses as stimulants to head-hunting, and to introduce missionaries and medical services, can only result in the destruction of the Asmat culture and of the delicately balanced relationship of the population with its environment. The intention is to make West Irian safe for tourist development.

I fear that for many of the 'problem people' of the world, who can neither face the ruthless power of the white man, nor accept his standards of civilization, the only prospect is to be stripped of all dignity and to be treated as archaic curiosities for the interest of uncomprehending tourists.

5 The Forbidden Kingdom

The Himalayas, extending across the north of the Indian sub-continent from Afghanistan to Burma, have always held a romantic attraction for me. As a schoolboy I learned the mystery-filled names of the highest peaks, convinced that they promised even greater delights than Rider Haggard's African Mountains of the Moon, which at that time were my only literary source of mountain lore and legend. In my romantic daydreams I not infrequently planted the Union Jack on the pinnacle of Everest, though I have to confess that in later life my own serious mountaineering was restricted to a single holiday in the Bernese Oberland, from which I returned without having gained any notable distinction.

Nevertheless, when I finally had the good fortune not only to see most of the highest mountains of the Himalayas, but to set foot on the slopes of several of them, I was impressed beyond my wildest dreams. In my mind's eye their glittering peaks remain distinct, each surrounded by the adventure of a journey. Nanga Parbat, which the Gilgitis call 'the mother of clouds', came first. Then the mysterious K 2, the second highest mountain in the world. Then Annapurna, vast and gleaming above the Pokhara Valley in Nepal; and Kanchenjunga, the world's third highest peak, seen from Sikkim, whose people regard it as the abode of gods. And supreme above them all, the immaculate 29,028-foot crest of Everest, which the Tibetans call Sagarmatha 'the mother goddess of the world', on whose flanks I spent three memorable days.

With fifty peaks exceeding 25,000 feet, ten of which are among the highest on earth, the Himalayas stagger the beholder by their sheer magnificence. How aptly they have been called the roof of the world! Yet in terms of the world's history they are still relatively young, having been formed between the late Miocene and late Pleistocene periods, that is to say between 1·5 and 10 million years ago. The best impression of the vastness of the range, which cuts off India from the high Tibetan Plateau like a never-ending wall, is to fly along it, preferably in a small plane whose pilot will keep well below the level of the peaks. But to appreciate the size of a mountain one needs comparative perspective. One must either attempt to climb its slopes, which in the case of the Himalayas is a task for supermen, or, as I have done on several occasions, take a small aircraft or a helicopter and fly within the peaks and land high up among them. There are places where a skilled pilot can do this with reasonable safety in suitable weather. Then only can one understand the real grandeur of the mountains and the physical stamina of those who succeed in climbing them. Even at a modest 13,000 feet which was as high as I ventured, the least exertion leaves the average middle-aged mortal gasping for breath and with a pounding heart.

It was not until 1954 that the first tourists were permitted to set foot in Nepal. Even at the time of my first visit in the early 1960s there were only fifty miles of permanent road in the Kingdom. Today, with new hotels in Kathmandu as luxurious as any in Asia and with a high-speed highway spanning the country from end to end about to be completed, Nepal has jumped in one bound from several thousand years of strict isolation into the hurly-burly of the jet age. What the effect of this sudden transition will be on the world's only Hindu Kingdom remains to be seen. The wind of change, while blowing away the cobwebs of the past, can also stir up unwelcome eddies. The days of the despotic Mallas and Shahs and of the autocratic Ranas were followed by the first faltering steps towards democracy. With the death of King Mahendra in 1972, modernity ascended the throne in the person of his son, the new young King Birendra, bringing with him a full knowledge of western technology and economics. The tradition-steeped and friendly people of Nepal, the Brahmins and Sherpas, the

Newars, the Bhotias, the Tamangs and the Gurungs, have never heard of such great mysteries as these.

Meanwhile, as soon as one leaves the outskirts of Kathmandu and enters the fertile alluvial lowlands of the terai, with its vivid mosaic of green and yellow paddyfields, one can still step back into the enchanting beauty of the past, to the wooden plough and the simple dignity of men whose lives are regulated by the sun and the monsoon. The terai, with its rich crops, is the life blood of Nepal and is the extremity of the fertile great plain of northern India. North of every prospect, from its entire length of nearly 500 miles across Nepal, shines the long frieze of the snowy Himalayan peaks. The only break in the range is the Kali Gandaki valley between the peaks of Annapurna and Dhaulagiri; but even this gap, which is much used by migrant birds from Tibet, is more than 14,000 feet above sea level.

Between the tropical terai and the mountains are the temperate foothills, where one begins to see the growing tragedy which threatens the once magnificent forests of Nepal. Here and on the mountain slopes, even in the Khumbu valleys around Everest, the forests are disappearing, replaced by mile upon mile of narrow terracing, constructed by superhuman effort for the growing of potatoes, maize, millet, barley, oats, or rice. Where pockets of hill forest remain, the trees are dying from being constantly denuded of branches for fuel, or of leaves for winter fodder for goats and cattle. Once malaria was brought under control in the terai, with the help of the World Health Organization, a southward migration of the hill people into the lowlands began and as each terraced hill farm was abandoned, the already severe erosion of the soil increased. Nepal is paying a heavy price for the loss of its protective montane forests, with their unique rhododendrons, azaleas, camellias, orchids and wildlife.

As a naturalist, I was less interested in the picturesque towns and villages of Nepal, with their countless pagodas, temples and stupas, than in the little known wildlife of the country. On my first visit I therefore obtained permission from King Mahendra to explore the remote western area of the terai, where tigers and other rare animals were said to be still relatively plentiful. His Majesty was genuinely interested in wildlife and anxious that the World Wildlife Fund, which I represented, should assist his government in devising effective conservation plans. A few years later both the King and Queen Ratna attended the tenth anniversary celebrations of the W.W.F. in Switzerland and I had the honour of introducing them to the Trustees. The new king's brother, H.R.H. Prince Gyanendra, has since then taken vigorous charge of Nepal's expanding conservation programme.

My guide on my first visit to the terai was Peter Byrne, who had lived for many years in Nepal and knew the wilder parts of the country intimately. Like many erstwhile hunters, he had eventually sold his guns and become an ardent conservationist. We planned to drive by Land-Rover from Kathmandu to the south-western corner of the terai near the Indian frontier. However, this ambitious proposal had to be abandoned when we learned that at least three river crossings were impassable on account of the late rains. All the rivers of Nepal flow southward across the terai, to feed the Ganges. There was nothing for it but to fly back to Delhi and attempt to enter the western terai from India.

The journey from Delhi required two days of hard driving. On the second day, having camped over-night at the roadside, we turned off the highway and followed the tracks of bullock-carts into the forest. After fording several rivers, we came to one which, in spite of our repeated efforts to climb the opposite bank, left us stranded in the water. A passing goat-herd summoned help from a farm, and by a combination of winching and digging away the steep bank, we were able to continue our journey. Night had again fallen before Peter announced, as we zig-zagged among the trees, that we had now crossed the un-marked frontier and were in Nepal. It was obvious that any poacher with Peter's uncanny navigational skill could also escape notice by the frontier guards. Indian poachers were known to be taking a heavy toll of Nepal's remaining tigers.

Only one more river had to be negotiated, this time in total darkness. I was pleased that on this occasion our headlights attracted a challenge from a Nepalese forest guard, an old friend of Peter's, who gave us a friendly welcome and let us pass. We finally halted inside what has now become the Sukla Phanta wildlife reserve (*see* Plate 4).

In remarkably few minutes, Peter's experienced Sherpa, who had accompanied us on the journey, had the tents pitched and a hot meal simmering over a blazing camp fire. A heavy dew was pattering drops of water on the crisp dry leaves beneath the teak tree under whose branches we were camping. Fifty yards away, under a layer of white mist, the Bamhani River was purling over its wide bed and in the distance a forest eagle owl was sounding its deep note at measured intervals. The moon had now risen and through a gap in the high leaf canopy we could see it shining benignly on the dark jungle.

After an admirable dinner of curried goat, we sat warming our toes by the fire, a bottle of whisky on the ground between us, while Peter talked about tigers. We were a very long way from civilization, in one of the most remote and beautiful regions of the world. As I lay on my cot later that night, I felt an indefinable sense of peace and well-being. Our open tent provided merely a top and back shelter from the dew. Around us the jungle was inky black except for the warm glow from the fire, about which an immense moth was circling on yellow velvet wings. I was just dropping off, when I was suddenly roused to complete alertness by the unmistakable distant roar of a tiger. My day was complete.

Dawn was even more wonderful than the night. The rising sun threw long horizontal shafts of light through the trees. Hidden in the high foliage, langur monkeys were leaping and jabbering. A pied hornbill clattered through the branches, setting to flight a host of green pigeons. Over the river the mist was dispersing and the sun gilding the feathery white blossoms of the reeds. The first kingfishers were flashing like living jewels over the mosaic of ethereal, lilac-blue water hyacinths in a backwater. A stately painted stork, a symphony in white with an obbligato of pink and black scalloping and with a shining yellow bill, stood mirrored in the green water, where a crimson-faced sarus crane was hunting for frogs, its woolly chick by its side. Junglecocks and peacocks were crowing all along the forest edge.

Walking back to camp for breakfast, Peter pointed to the sandy ground, where, perfectly imprinted, were the obviously fresh pug-marks of a large tigress. The mark of the pad of the female is distinguished by being less close to the toes than in the male. The tracks led behind our tent and in a circle around the camp. I was sufficiently impressed to measure the distance from my cot to the nearest tracks. It was only twenty-four feet.

'She was just curious,' said Peter. 'Probably attracted by the smell of the goat meat.'

Nepal used to be famous for its tigers, which under the old régime provided abundant sport for the rulers. By modern standards the method of hunting was barbarous. Several hundred elephants converged on an area known to contain tigers, until they formed a solid ring, which was then sealed by a cloth barrier in front of the elephants. The tigers were shot down as they tried to break out. Much greater losses have since been caused by the progressive destruction of tiger habitat and by commercially sponsored poaching from northern India, which includes the use of poisoned bait. The number of tigers now surviving in Nepal probably does not exceed 150. Although they are now protected in the Sukla Phanta, Karnali and Chitawan reserves, some poaching, alas, continues.

After breakfast we waded across the Bamhani River and walked into the forest, until we came to an open area of high grass where again and again we disturbed flocks of peafowl and groups of various deer resting after their night's feeding. The deer were mainly barasingha, the big marsh deer which have now become very rare. There are a few in the Indian States of Madhya Pradesh and Uttar Pradesh and in the Kaziranga reserve in Assam, but the largest surviving population, about one thousand animals, is in Sukla Phanta. They are beautiful creatures, not unlike the Scottish red deer, the stags carrying splendid antlers of up to fourteen points, with single curved brow-tines.

As the temperature rose, we headed back into the shade of the jungle, where we soon found ourselves having to wade numerous streams among thickets of 20-foot elephant grass and bamboo. The evil-smelling mud in the stream beds was as soft as butter and before long we were soaked to the waist. I called a halt in order to wring out my trousers and, to Peter's huge amusement, found my under-pants soaked with blood extracted by seven enormous leeches, which hung like ripe plums from my body. Remembering my frequent encounters with these noisome pests during the Burma campaign, I applied a lighted cigarette to the tails of those which did not drop off, to make them release their suckers, and we went on our way.

A little later, when we paused for a moment on higher ground, we heard stealthy movements in a clump of high grass and Peter signalled me to keep silent. Again the rustle of a large body and a movement in the thicket, this time to our left. Peter whispered, 'Tiger.' I felt my adrenalin surging. We were unarmed except for the Gurkha *kukri* knife hanging from Peter's belt and there were no climbable trees near us. Silence — and then a puffing sigh, followed by the sound of dry vegetation being crushed under a heavy weight.

After waiting for a while Peter said, 'Come on, it's probably gone to lie-up after a good meal.' Although my confidence in his knowledge of tigers was great, I could not resist a backward glance as we picked our way quietly into the jungle again. It was only later, when I had more experience of tiger-watching in India, Bangladesh and Nepal, that I realized how much tigers preferred to avoid contact with man unless openly provoked, or no longer able, from wounds or old age, to hunt their natural prey.

The remainder of our journey back to camp was uneventful, apart from a two-hour spell when we lost the elephant track we were following and had to hack our way through the maze of thickets. The welcome smudge of blue smoke from our camp eventually came into view. Muddy to the eyebrows and exhausted, I found with joy that our Sherpa had rigged up a shower with a perforated bucket hanging from a tree. I stripped and let the cold water run down me, still in a state of blissful euphoria from my first day in the Nepalese terai.

6 *The Men of the Mountains*

It was by a strange quirk of fortune that after exploring the Rift Valley in Jordan, which at 1,298 feet below sea level in the Dead Sea area is the lowest spot on earth, I next found myself engaged in a similar task among the world's highest mountains.

There is something about the people of the high mountain communities of the Himalayas which one does not feel with the gregarious inhabitants of the lowlands. A sense not only of physical and cultural isolation, but of stubborn determination to resist the modern world. I sensed this particularly when I was exploring some of the high valleys of the Karakoram Range, in the course of the World Wildlife Fund expedition to Pakistan in 1967.

For this period of our work we made our base at Gilgit, a little town which could scarcely be more isolated from outside influences. It can be reached by road through the 13,500-foot Babusar Pass, which, on account of snow or rockfalls, is open, on average, for only thirty-six days in the year. Or, when the weather is favourable, which is not very often, an aircraft can land on Gilgit's small airstrip, high among the usually cloud-covered mountains, We were fortunate in having good weather for our flight and I was able to photograph the serrated 26,660-foot crest of Nanga Parbat as we approached. Down one side of this great mountain flows one of the largest glaciers in the world. Beyond lay Mount Rakoposhi, which the Gilgitis call 'the mother of clouds' and on our left the frowning mass of the Hindu Kush, where the frontiers of the USSR, China and Pakistan meet. Our aircraft, provided by the Pakistan government, then dived down through the clouds into the trench of the Gilgit valley and landed on the runway, stopping with its nose uncomfortably close to the high mountain which rises like a wall at the far end.

We had timed our visit to take advantage of the fine spell which normally precedes the first snow around mid-November. Even so, our return journey was delayed by three days of persistent snow clouds and we were fortunate to be able to hitchhike our way back to Lahore on a military plane which braved the bad visibility. A short time afterwards a similar aircraft tried to get out and hit a cloud-covered mountain, killing all twenty-six passengers.

The Gilgit Agency, established by the British in 1889, has had a turbulent history. Ptolemy was apparently the first to describe the warlike Dards, as its original inhabitants were called. The Chinese pilgrim Hsuan Tsang, who ascended to Gilgit from Swat in AD 631, wrote: 'Perilous were the roads and dark the gorges . . . here were ledges hanging in mid-air; there flying bridges over abysses; elsewhere paths cut with the chisel, or mere footings to climb by'. More than thirteen hundred years later, this description of travel in the Gilgit Agency is still no exaggeration. The few mountain roads were made for agile mules, not motor-cars.

According to its rather hazy early history, Gilgit was first ruled by the Rajas of Trakane. A long succession of foreign invasions followed. In 1846 Kashmir and Gilgit were placed by the British under the rule of Gulab Singh of Jammu, Maharaja of the Dogras. The fierce Dards staged an uprising in 1852 and massacred the entire army of occupation in Gilgit, which they held until 1889, when the British took control to forestall an advance by Russia. When Britain withdrew from the Indian subcontinent in 1947, a Kashmiri Governor was unwisely appointed to Gilgit. The famous Gilgit Scouts, originally raised as the Hunza Levies by General Sir George Cockerill and regarded as a *corps d'élite*, instantly revolted and proclaimed accession to the new nation of Pakistan.

The Agency embraces a number of small principalities between the borders of Chitral, Afghanistan, the USSR and the Chinese province of Sinkiang. Though the Shins are now the dominant race and theirs the language most spoken, there are many others. The typical costume of the Gilgitis is a long felt coat called a *chogha*, with sleeves reaching below the knees; in cold weather they are wrapped around the neck as a scarf. Baggy pyjama trousers are tucked into puttees. A distinctive, close-fitting cap called a *khoi* is worn with the soft brim rolled into a kind of sausage around the head. The women, who in this essentially rugged man's world live lives of unremitting toil, wear brimless, pill-box caps. Money is little used, most of the trade being on a basis of barter between the producers of foodstuffs and livestock.

There is a timelessness about the enclosed valleys of Gilgit which the presence of intruders such as ourselves, with our modern paraphernalia of jeeps, cameras and binoculars, only heightened. In the very few villages through which we passed during our explorations, the women looked up only briefly from their work, their expressions neither welcoming, curious nor resentful. Their occupations were as they had been for centuries, wielding heavy hoes in the stony fields, drawing water, lopping the branches of willows or walnut trees for fuel and winter fodder, weaving wool, milking goats, or stacking hay in the trees to keep it out of reach of the goats. We rarely saw men in the villages, though we occasionally passed one on horseback, or caught sight of one watching us from a mountainside, sitting hawk-like on a rock with a rifle across his knees. At dawn each morning, when we were staying at the rest-house in Gilgit, a straggling line of prisoners from the local gaol clanked past in leg-irons on their way to work in the fields under armed guard. We were told that they were all murderers, fatalities arising from disputes over land or women being commonplace in the valleys. The only animated scene was in the Gilgit market, where picturesquely dressed traders sat cross-legged in their stalls, haggling over the prices of skins, carpets, cooking-pots, clothing, foodstuffs, or weapons made by the skilful back-street gunsmiths of Peshawar or Kohat.

On our first day in Gilgit we were invited to the finals of the local polo tournament and I was asked by the Resident Governor to throw the first ball. The Gilgitis claim to have invented polo, though in fact it originated in Persia. Their version of the game is, however, an astonishing and unique spectacle. It gives the impression of a kind of equestrian rugby football, played without any perceptible restraint. There is apparently only one rule: play must be continuous until one side has scored nine goals, or until one hour has elapsed. There is no nonsense about changing ponies between chukkas, nor any rules to protect riders or their mounts from injury. Because of the scarcity of flat ground in the valleys, the stony polo fields are small and narrow and are enclosed by stone walls, into which players drive their opponents at full gallop. A player may catch the ball in mid-air and ride with it into goal, but at the risk of having his hand smashed by a polo stick, or of being dragged bodily from his pony and dropped among the flying hooves. Injuries to players and ponies are frequent, but are not allowed to halt the game. Every valley has its team and small boys in the villages play a pedestrian version, using a stone instead of a ball.

At the match which we attended, several thousand picturesquely dressed hill tribesmen crowded every inch of the mountainside, keeping up a deafening roar of encouragement to their favourite teams. For sheer excitement, I know of only one other equestrian game which can compare with Gilgit polo and that is *buzkashi*, as played in Afghanistan; but instead of using a ball, the Afghan horsemen fight for possession of the carcass of a goat.

In the course of the following two weeks we explored the valleys, sleeping in primitive rest-houses or village schools. Everywhere we were received with courtesy. Men with whom we talked were neither haughty nor deferential; they looked us in the eye in a manner of calm but gracious kinship. Local dignitaries often invited us to their homes. Such visits enabled us to learn something about the difficulties of life in such an isolated region. Every journey was an adventure, the narrow mountain roads twisting among awe-inspiring gorges. Often the gradients were one in three, or, in places, even one in two, so that our jeeps were continually kept in four-wheel drive.

When we met cattle or, on rare occasions, other vehicles, it was necessary to back the jeeps round the innumerable hairpin bends above precipices, until there was sufficient room to squeeze past. In many places the road edge had crumbled away and been rebuilt merely by piling up uncemented boulders which were revetted with twisted juniper logs. It required courage to take the jeeps over these hazards when their collapse might involve plunging for fifteen hundred feet into the river below. Sometimes, after driving for hours, we had to turn back because a landslide had carried away the road, or buried it. Often the road zig-zagged repeatedly back and forth over a gorge on a series of fragile wooden suspension bridges, which creaked and undulated even under the weight of a single pedestrian. They were invariably constructed at a sharp right angle to the road and the utmost care was needed, in turning the jeeps on to them, not to carry away the wooden handrails. At the head of the Naltar Valley we ran into snow at 11,000 feet and had to man-handle the jeeps. On another occasion we even had to lift one bodily back on to the track when two of its wheels went over the edge.

Driving back from Naltar we passed a party of Gujars, the nomads who spend the summer in the high alpine meadows of the Himalayas and Kashmir, driving their flocks down to the valleys for the winter. All their oxen, horses and women were carrying enormous loads of tentage and household chattels and even the small children were walking barefoot in the snow. Many of the men appeared to have Mongoloid features, quite unlike the proud, hawk-nosed faces of the Gilgit mountain people, and were as wild a lot of brigands as we had seen anywhere. All carried guns and long knives with decorative sheaths.

We spent one night at the head of the Gupis Valley, only a few miles from the Chinese frontier. Up to the time of the First World War, this was the northernmost outpost of the British Army in India. In those days there was a little fortress, where the garrison defended the pass with two muzzle-loaded screw-guns. It is a bleak and forbidding area, with a rainfall of only three inches a year. Our lips were chapped by the bitter wind which howled down from the icefields beyond. But the kindly Raja of Gupis had sent green tea and little cakes to welcome us at the rest-house and we soon had an aromatic fire of juniper logs burning in the snug living-room.

We spent that evening with the local doctor. His little house, sturdily built to withstand the long Himalayan winter, reminded me of a Russian *dacha*; in the centre of the room was a pot-bellied iron stove, with a samovar bubbling contentedly on top. We dined by the soft glow of oil lamps.

Gupis is a tiny village and most of the doctor's patients lived in mobile camps to be near their cattle during the summer, descending to the village only when driven down by snow. There was, however, a small hospital, which served a very large area. When the roads were closed in winter, the doctor had to deal with every emergency on foot and single handed. The women of the mountain people were forbidden to expose their bodies to a stranger and could therefore be treated only through relatives. Childbirth requiring Caesarean operation invariably led to an agonizing death and epidemics were uncontrollable. Although the people were extremely hardy, illness arising from dietary deficiency was frequent, as were tuberculosis, jaundice and eye complaints such as cataract and trachoma. The doctor described his work dispassionately and without complaint, though his life must have been an almost unbearably lonely one.

We breakfasted next morning with the Raja of Gupis, an elderly man of great charm and dignity dressed in the traditional embroidered *choga*, with sleeves almost reaching the ground. He was very well informed about the larger animals of the mountains which we were studying. All of them had suffered severe losses from uncontrolled hunting, not only by the local tribesmen, who shot them for food or to protect their flocks, but by the military and visiting VIPs from Rawalpindi and Lahore. The chief game animals were the magnificent local race of the markhor goat, which has distinctively widespread spiral horns, the ibex, the shapu wild sheep and the massively-horned Marco Polo's sheep. A heavy toll was also being taken of the snow leopards, leopard cats, lynxes and black bears. Though regretting the gradual disappearance of these animals, the Raja told us he still paid a bounty in grain for every snow leopard or wolf shot, trapped, or poisoned, because of their habit of raiding the goat flocks. We had already observed that there were far too many goats, which were not only destroying the sparse grazing up to altitudes of 14,000 feet and thereby depriving the wild ungulates of their food, but had also been responsible for introducing anthrax into the markhor and shapu populations. Here, as in the Middle East, Africa and South America, the domestic goat was the arch enemy of conservation.

I asked the Raja to explain the barter system practised at Gupis. It was a simple matter, he said. The rates of exchange were decided at meetings with the village elders according to the availability or scarcity of commodities. At the present time one goat was worth twenty-eight pounds of grain. Twenty pounds of grain could be exchanged for two and a half pounds of butter. Two female goats were worth one good male and six goats one cow. Two cows would buy one ploughing bullock and three bullocks one polo pony. It seemed a very practical arrangement where money had little significance. Very few of the men of Gupis had ever felt the need to make the long and arduous journey across the mountains and down to the cities in the hot plains of the Indus. Gupis was a poor community and, because the laws of inheritance were based not on primogeniture but on an equal division between all the sons, land was constantly being broken up into smaller and smaller parcels. Asked why the laws of inheritance were not changed, the Raja smiled gently and said, 'Traditions are very strong in the mountains.' Thinking of the tradition which condemned women to die in agony rather than be seen by a doctor, I felt sad for the proud people of Gupis.

Soon after leaving Gupis, where the road followed the river-bed, we noticed in the wide flood-track several large boulders covered with chiselled graffiti. Inspection revealed them to represent designs of men with bows and arrows, shooting at very recognizable ibex, markhor, snow leopard and lynx, Judging by the weathering of the rocks, we thought the designs were probably either Neolithic or Palaeolithic. We had found

similar graffiti on a journey to Phandar Lake, which lies at
10,500 feet above sea level half a day's journey from Gupis,
but these had included men on horseback, shooting backwards
with crossbows, in the manner usually ascribed to the Phoeni-
cians. We longed for an archaeologist to unravel their fascinating clues to the prehistory of the Gilgit Agency.

A few days later we called on the Raja of Punial, another of
the local hereditary princes, whose territory lies at the junction
of the Ishkoman Valley and the high peaks of Hunza. The
approach to the Raja's house, which was guarded by a small
medieval fort, was dramatic. After descending twenty-one
hairpin bends down the mountain road, we came to a raging
torrent, which we crossed by a narrow wooden bridge leading
to a courtyard. On one side was the little fort and on the other
a small, fairly modern house where the Raja lived. We learned
later that in the days of the Raja's grandfather, the bridge had
been a fragile affair of rope woven from the bark of trees. The
old Raja was apparently a great practical joker. One of his
favourite tricks was to wait until a guest was half-way across
the bridge and then cut the main rope with an axe, dropping
him into the torrent. We received a much more hospitable
welcome. The valley of Punial, known locally as 'the place
where heaven and earth meet' is extremely beautiful and certainly lives up to its name.

The Raja spoke excellent English. He had a large grey
moustache and but for his dress could have passed for a typical
Edwardian county squire. Once a keen hunter, he now devoted
himself to farming and the problems of his small domain. His
house was comfortable and full of character, but totally lacking
any trace of the extravagant splendour which one used to
associate with the hereditary princes of the subcontinent. Over
the mantelpiece was an enlarged photograph of his fun-loving
grandfather, taken at the turn of the century, an impressive
figure with a fierce black beard and a curved sabre, in traditional Gilgit costume and cross-over puttees.

After an admirable lunch we walked in the sunny gardens,
where domestic poultry and geese were feeding contentedly
among the beds of zinnias and marigolds. The Raja was an

excellent naturalist and able to provide us with valuable information about the behaviour of snow leopards, which he now watched with pleasure instead of shooting them. When, as dusk approached, we took our leave, he showed us a Russian ring removed from the leg of a greylag goose, which he had shot in 1966. We were able afterwards to trace its origin. It had been ringed as a juvenile in 1959 at Chatyr Kul Lake in Kirgiz S.S.R. and had obviously crossed the high Himalayas on its way to Punial.

One of the most remarkable people we met during our exploration in the Gilgit valleys was an old *shikari*, who attached himself to our party one day when we were looking for markhor. He was reputed to be the local expert on the behaviour of these very shy animals and to know exactly where we could best observe them. When I first met him I was astonished by his appearance. He was obviously very old and wizened and his tattered *choga* hung on his sparse frame as on a clotheshorse. But his toothless grin and twinkling eyes were so appealing that I agreed to take him with us, without believing that he could be of much use. He advised us to drive to Kargah Nullah and to arrive in the late afternoon, when the markhor would descend to drink in the river.

We reached the yawning gorge by three o'clock. Where to stop was decided for us by reaching a point where the entire road had been obliterated by a huge landslide some 300 yards wide. After surveying the scene with expert eyes, the old *shikari* pointed to a projecting spur of rock about 1,500 feet above us which, he said, would be an admirable spot from which to see the markhor. He said this with complete confidence and without more ado set off straight up the steep mountainside at a fast pace. He was wearing thin and badly tattered sandals on his bare feet, but seemed to scale the broken rocks as though they were carpeted stairs, reaching the pinnacle long before any of us. I arrived last and exhausted. I have always loved mountains, but climbing at the 10,000-foot level imposes a certain strain even on the young; on the eve of my sixty-second birthday I was, alas, no longer able to climb with the easy gusto of my youth. From our vantage point, our jeeps looked like miniature toys far below by the narrow ribbon of the river.

The tremendous cliff opposite us was honeycombed with wind-eroded caves, in which the markhor often sheltered during snowstorms. The sun was now well down and the light failing behind heavy clouds. It was bitterly cold and a strong wind bearing sleet was whistling around the promontory, forcing us back into the shelter of the rocks. Our *shikari*, however, lay full length on the edge of the jutting rock, his eyes glued to the binoculars I had lent him, apparently impervious to the cold.

Half an hour later he gave an exclamation of triumph. Far above on the opposite cliff he had spotted a group of markhor coming almost vertically down a fissure in the rocks. Soon afterwards a large, bearded male, followed by four females, came over the skyline to our left. I was able to see that the male had great corkscrew horns of fully forty inches and a coat of long grey hair almost to his knees.

In the failing light and against the wilderness of grey, broken rocks, it was almost unbelievable that the old man had spotted the animals at a distance of more than a quarter of a mile. We descended to our vehicles delighted by his prowess. When we dropped him off at Gilgit he refused the offer of payment, though gladly taking cigarettes. Through our interpreter I asked him his age. With a toothless grin he replied, "I am ninety years old." Whether this was true or not, he was a remarkable advertisement for the skill and hardihood of the men of Gilgit.

Following our recommendations to the Pakistan Government, the whole of this romantic region and its unique wildlife is now scheduled for development as a protected national park, under the auspices of the Pakistan branch of the World Wildlife Fund.

7　A Walk in the Barrens

Most of us instinctively feel happier and more at ease in certain surroundings and climates than in others. Your hardy Scot has little admiration for the balmy air and softly rounded green hills of southern England. For him the wild bubbling cry of a curlew high in the heather is infinitely more precious than the contralto song of a nightingale in a Sussex copse. There is something in our heredity which dictates these things. While I can appreciate the austere beauty of the Canadian Arctic or the high northern forests of Finnish Lapland, I feel a greater spiritual contentment in warm or hot climates. Providing one is properly equipped, the northern barrens are, of course, in reality no more hostile to man than the arid zones of the world, yet I feel more of an intruder in them than I do in deserts. I have been temporarily lost in both and on each occasion by my own stupidity. The experience was salutary. It taught me to appreciate the skill in orientation of the human inhabitants of such regions, who spend their lives with no more guidance than the sun or stars.

Watching wildlife rarely encourages one to take a straight course across country. There are always intriguing sights to lead one astray. Where there are no landmarks, as in the tundra or in deserts, a compass becomes a necessity to those not born in such lands. I had only myself to blame when one day I left camp in the Norwegian tundra without remembering this precaution.

I had been camping with a Norwegian friend who had returned to his university with the promise of rejoining me at the weekend. Our camp in a patch of stunted birches was on the edge of one of the large areas of tundra which are scattered in a long chain up the northern part of Norway beyond the Arctic Circle. It was mid-summer and, though cold, the sun was shining from an almost cloudless sky when I set out. I wanted to find the nest of some cranes which my friend said were probably breeding in the bogs a few miles from our camp.

I took a north-westerly course across the tundra, which stretched without interruption of any kind to the horizon. In the morning sun its uniformly grey surface of lichens and reindeer moss was shining with light reflected from thousands of small pools and the sky was full of ducks and waders criss-crossing between them. On every side there were pleasant distractions. Here a pair of tortoiseshell-coloured turnstones were nesting, there some red-necked phalaropes were spinning on the surface of a pool to stir up the food for their young. Lapland buntings and dainty bluethroats were darting among the tussocks and patches of hairy pasque flowers, which the Norwegians called 'mogops'. The ground was uniformly spongy and at each step my gumboots sank into water from three to ten inches deep. I carried a five-foot thumbstick, with which I probed the ground ahead of me. So long as I could feel the ice beneath the deep mat of mosses I could walk safely, though the moss undulated on its cushion of water at every step. It was rather like walking on a trampoline. Where the ice had thawed, I had to retreat and take a different direction to circumvent these treacherous holes. I was in a typical glacial plain. The occasional breaks in the hidden ice over the permanently frozen subsoil, or permafrost, are what the geologists call 'kettle-holes'. The open pools, however, were a delight, as they were swarming with birds such as wood sandpipers, spotted redshanks, golden plovers, dunlins and Temminck's stints.

The little black mosquitoes and biting flies of the tundra, which are such a trial to humans, are a boon to the northern willow warblers and other insectivorous birds which inhabit the bogs. In spite of the insect repellant with which I had smeared my hands and face, I was constantly coated with these tiresome pests, though they did not bite me.

As I trudged along, I thought about the tundra, this wild, bleak region which even in the brief mild summer looked to the layman so empty, yet which in reality teemed with myriad life-forms. For most of the year it was a frozen, twilight wilderness, scoured by the blast of icy winds and snow, under which all life cringed, dormant and immobile. But when the thaw came, life again exploded from the earth, to blossom, to metamorphose, to reproduce, with an urgency rivalled only by the response of a long-parched desert to the first rains. Then from far and wide poured in the migrant birds, to feast on the abundance of insect life, to nest and to raise their young in haste before the first breath of the long winter blasted the tundra once again. For all its rugged appearance, its vegetation is extremely fragile. And the farther north one goes, the more vulnerable the mosses become. Studies in the barrens of Alaska during the long controversy over the laying of oil pipelines showed that the slightest damage to the moss cushions takes an extraordinarily long time to recover. A small party of men walking a track regularly for a few months can destroy the moss completely, leaving only bare earth. A similar study in the alpine tundra of the Rocky Mountains revealed that even the weight of an empty beer-can tossed into the living moss can leave a scar which takes many months to recover. The tundra is a harsh yet tender world.

After more than three hours of steady if zig-zag walking, I found the cranes. They had spotted me the moment my head came above the horizon and they led me, by their behaviour, to their nest in a marshy hollow. As I drew nearer, both birds began elaborate distraction displays, alighting and running with long strides in a curiously crouched attitude and croaking loudly, in the hope of tempting me to follow a 'wounded' bird. It was very similar to the 'broken wing' distraction behaviour of a ringed plover, when it tries to draw an intruder away from its nest.

The cranes would not return to their eggs cradled in the heap of damp vegetation so long as I was visible. One of the eggs was chipping and I could see the pink tip of the nestling's bill working at the hole it had made in the shell. So I withdrew, closely followed for half an hour by one of the agitated cranes.

It was very tiring walking in the bogs and I decided to make for the slightly higher ground in the distance, in the hope of finding somewhere dry where I could eat my lunch. By the time I reached it, I had been walking for more than four hours. Sitting on my rucksack, for the moss was still wet even on higher ground, I had a leisurely meal of corned beef sandwiches and chocolate while I surveyed my surroundings. I rather expected to be able to pick out the little clump of eight-foot birches by my camp with my binoculars, but although the plain was as flat as the proverbial pancake on all sides, the horizon was empty. I did not anticipate any difficulty in locating the camp, however, on my return journey.

From my vantage point I was able to see plenty of wildlife. A moving spot of white on my right turned out to be a northern hare which had only partially shed its white winter coat, leaving it amusingly piebald but dangerously vulnerable to its predators. At this latitude there should have been reindeer feeding on the rich crop of mosses, but I saw none that day. To my left, however, I noticed a long-winged bird with a heavy, rounded head, quartering the ground in purposeful manner. It was certainly neither a rough-legged buzzard nor a short-eared owl, both of which I had already noticed over the tundra. Shouldering my rucksack again, I went for a closer look. The bird led me on for half an hour before I got close enough to determine that it was one of the most romantic birds of the north — the great grey, or Lapland, owl. This splendid creature, almost as large as an eagle owl, has, for an owl, uncommonly small yellow eyes set in large, concentrically-ringed facial discs, which give it a very fierce expression. Normally an inhabitant of coniferous forests, it had evidently been tempted to hunt in the open tundra by the large numbers of lemmings which were present that year.

Feeling by now rather fatigued by my laborious progress through the quaking bogs, I headed back towards my camp. The countless pools which I had to circumnavigate and from each of which fresh clouds of mosquitoes rose to torment me, now began to take a greater toll on my stamina. Having no outstanding feature to guide me, I kept the sun on my right and maintained as straight a south-easterly course as the pools permitted. A chill wind was now blowing in my face and the sky was becoming overcast.

After two hours of steady plodding, I stopped to rest and to drink the last of the coffee in my thermos flask. I calculated that I had about another three hours to go before reaching camp. I had by now discovered that I had left my compass in my tent, but was not unduly worried by this, as the clump of birch trees would be clearly visible for at least half a mile. Two and a half hours later, however, I began to wonder whether my usually good sense of direction had let me down. The horizon ahead of me was still completely unbroken. There was no change in the scene except that the pools seemed more numerous than ever. The sun was now well down and the temperature was dropping. Although I was perspiring freely from my exertions, the cold wind on my sodden trousers was unpleasant. In the middle of this limitless, wet wilderness I suddenly felt vulnerable. Its vastness made me feel as though I had shrunk to the size of an ant. I made careful calculations of time and distance, allowing for stops, and decided that if I did not see the camp within another hour's walking, I would probably have passed beyond it, assuming my direction to have been correct. I reckoned that my rate of progress was rather less than two miles an hour.

When after an hour there was still no sign of the birch trees, I erected a marker with clumps of tussocks pulled from the ground and struck off at right angles to the left of the direction I had been following. Taking careful note of any distinctive feature as I went, so that I could find my way back, I continued for one hour in that direction. Coming eventually to a large pond which I was sure I would have noticed had I passed it before, and seeing nothing familiar ahead, I then retraced my steps to the marker. After half an hour's rest, I set off again in the opposite direction for one hour. This, too, proved fruitless and the tundra continued to extend in an unbroken line ahead.

I was by now aching in every limb and very tired. My feet

felt heavier every time I dragged them out of the bog. Although it was many hours since I had finished the last of my food, I fortunately still had plenty of tobacco and after smoking a pipe I went back to the marker. By the time I reached it, it was midnight and the Arctic sun hung like a sullen orange ball near the horizon, poised before the advent of the new day. The sky was peach-coloured around it, but a dull, steely grey elsewhere. Over the tundra there was now little sign of bird life in the curious light, which was neither dusk nor full daylight. Apart from the bluethroats, which still sang snatches of their tinkling, silver-bell songs among the tussocks, all was quiet, though it was difficult to believe that it was the middle of the night. I poured the water from my boots and lay down on the wet moss to consider what to do next. There was no chance whatever that anyone would pass within sight and I was still half a day's walking from the nearest road beyond the camp. I felt certain that I was not such a bad navigator as to have been completely mistaken in my sense of direction when I had set out on my return journey. With my binoculars, I had been able to sweep a huge area to right and left of the marker over a total distance of perhaps six miles. There remained only two possibilities — either I had headed in the wrong direction from the start, or I had misjudged the distance covered on my outward journey and had halted too soon on my return. The latter seemed the more likely, in which case the camp still lay ahead.

Satisfied by this deduction, I dozed for half an hour, until the cold and the dampness brought me to my feet again.

After slaking my thirst from a brackish pool, I set off briskly forward from the marker. The sun was now rising again and the light was bright. Snipe were flying from the pools and drumming overhead in long, oblique power-dives, with tails widely spread. An Arctic fox loped away ahead of me and everywhere birds were active again. It was another day.

Little more than a mile of steady walking brought me to firmer ground and suddenly I saw a slight bump on the horizon to my left. Through my binoculars the little birch trees of the camp were clearly visible. Had I continued the previous day in a straight line for another half hour, I would have saved myself from what had been a very unpleasant experience. Since lunch that day I had struggled through the quaking bogs for nearly twelve hours.

A steaming billycan of baked beans and bacon had never tasted so good as it did that morning when I reached camp. But, as I said earlier, I had learned a salutary lesson.

8 Beauty and the Beast

Night-time in the Sunderbans. The setting moon hangs low over the Pussur River, which slides, glass-smooth on its way to the Bay of Bengal between the overhanging sundri trees and the graceful golpatta palms. The tide is ebbing, exposing along the muddy shores a million sharp bayonets — the spike-like pneumatophores, or air-roots, by which the mangroves obtain the life-giving oxygen which they cannot extract from the muddy, saline water. Among the regiments of spikes, fiddler crabs are already excavating their holes and waving their monstrously enlarged single claws. The little amphibian mud-skipper fish, too, are beginning to exchange the comparative safety of the river for the more dangerous element of the open air as dawn approaches, rowing themselves forward on the wet mud with their limb-like pectoral fins. But the junglecocks, the true heralds of day, have not yet begun to crow and the stillness of night is broken only by the high, nervous bark of a chital stag.

Tied up near the bank is a slender canoe, its sleeping occupant shrouded against the heavy dew. He has paddled all day from his little stilted bamboo hut in Chandpai village to reach this spot. Tomorrow he will join his companions on the ancient fishing boat with the carved prow lying in the shallows near Tiger Point. He has seven children and is desperately poor. Like his companions, he is deeply in debt to the *mahajans*, the rich moneylenders to whom the catch is always mortgaged in advance at usurious rates of interest. When his daughters marry he will borrow again for their dowries. When he dies, his debts will be passed on to his sons and they, too, will probably be in debt all their lives. It is the custom and beyond complaining.

Again the chital barks and stamps. It scents danger. Minutes pass and in the failing moonlight near where the canoe is tied, the massive head of a tiger materializes under the arching branches. The cold greenish eyes are on the canoe and the white-spotted ears are pricked forward. Noiselessly, placing its great paws with precision between the sharp pneumato-phores, the tiger advances to the water's edge, calculating the distance. A safe twenty feet of water separated the canoe from the bank when it was tied up at dusk. Barely nine feet of water now remain. The tiger crouches, its feet deep in the mud, and with an easy leap is in the canoe, which nearly capsizes under the 400-pound onslaught. There is a brief muffled cry and the tiger wades ashore, carrying the limp body of the fisherman by the neck, as nonchalantly as if it had been a goat. Fifty yards inside the shelter of the trees it drops the body and begins eating it, starting as usual on the buttocks.

A few weeks later, a patrolling forest guard notices the empty canoe and lands to investigate. The track where the body was dragged it still visible and in the little clearing is the fisherman's bloodstained and tattered *lungi*. Scavengers have removed what the tiger did not eat. When, a few days later, the guard reaches a telephone, he reports his discovery to the police and the Department of Forests at Khulna. Careful entries are made on official forms about the unknown fisher-man who became a victim of the man-eaters of the Sunder-bans. An officially recognized victim, that is, for empty canoes are often found in the vast wilderness of mangroves. Some of their occupants are doubtless killed by tigers, but unless there is evidence these do not appear in the statistics. Men can die without trace by many different means in these parts, from family feuds or drowning, to snake-bites or piracy.

I wrote this brief account of an incident in the Sunderbans soon after returning from my first visit there and came across it again recently when going through my files. I remember feeling that I wanted to commit to paper the impression made on me at the time. But looking back I find it impossible adequately to describe the mysterious, ever-changing Sunderbans. As Antoine de Saint Exupéry said of love, it is like a face perceived but never really seen. It guards its secrets jealously and perhaps one literally cannot see the wood for the trees, for it is densely clothed with jungle, stretching for 3,500 square miles across the delta of the Ganges and Brahmaputra. The only long views are down its countless twisting waterways, which day after day lead one deeper into the green wilderness. But around every bend is a new enchantment, or a new adventure. Immaculate white-bellied fishing eagles gaze down imperiously from the trees; heavily-tusked wild boar scamper away as one approaches; a 16-foot estuarine crocodile slips silently into the water until only its baleful yellow eyes are visible; a crested serpent eagle rises from the shore with a still wriggling cobra in its talons; a band of macaque monkeys chatters derisively from a pendant bough, where purple sunbirds are glinting among the orange vine blossoms . . . and everywhere the gleaming splendour of kingfishers, not one species but nine, ranging from the minute, violet three-toed to the flamboyantly coloured stork-billed, as large as a pigeon and with a grotesquely huge scarlet bill.

In the course of my wildlife survey for the Pakistan Government, and before the Sunderbans became part of Bangladesh, I passed several weeks in this wonderland, exploring the labyrinth of creeks and rivers. South of Chandpai, where harnessed otters are still used for driving fish into nets, there are no human habitations except for one or two high-stilted huts of the lonely forest guards. Hundreds of Bengali fishermen sail their picturesque boats down the main channels to the rich fishing grounds in the Bay of Bengal; but the only people brave enough ever to venture ashore are the honey-collectors and woodsmen. The tidal flooding and absence of high ground have protected the Sunderbans from the torrent of human numbers which has swept away so many of the wilderness areas of Asia. In consequence it still has a rich and varied population of wildlife, only the rhinoceros, the gaur jungle bison and the big barasingha marsh deer having been exterminated by hunters. Uncontrolled hunting reduced the once very large number of tigers to about 100 by 1965, but this is nevertheless the largest contiguous population remaining in the subcontinent. As such, it has particular value to science and the Sunderbans has now become a protected national park.

The word Sunderbans means 'beautiful forest'. Seen from the safety of a motor launch in the period between the monsoons, which was as I first saw it, the name could not be more appropriate. Yet to the Bengali fishermen who traverse it and to the several million simple villagers who live around its northern borders, it is a place of many tragedies and an ever-present threat of disaster. When the skies turn blue-black and fill with lightning and a cyclone races in from the Bay of Bengal, a solid wall of water crashes irresistibly through the Sunderbans, sweeping everything before it. Whole villages far to the north disappear without trace and the loss of life can be appalling. The hardy forests, evolved in a saline environment, are quick to recover, but in each recurrent cyclone the populations of land animals are almost wiped out and they take many years to recover. But for the fact that the tigers of the Sunderbans live aquatically, swimming from island to island and climbing trees more readily than their mainland counterparts, very few could have survived the terrible cyclone of 1969, when thousands of deer and wild boar perished. Only six tigers were found drowned.

Apart from cyclonic disasters, however, human life is also at risk in those parts of the Sunderbans where tigers have taken to man-killing. Nowhere else in the whole subcontinent has this habit been so persistent as here: indeed it is known to have been established as far back as the seventeenth century. Normally tigers, like any other wild creature, are only too anxious to avoid man and are not inherently aggressive towards him. If they take to man-killing it is nearly always because they are too infirm to hunt their natural prey, or have been wounded. It is significant that one of the Sunderbans tigers which recently claimed the lives of five men was found, when shot, to be both lame and very emaciated. Except for the Sunderbans, man-killing and man-eating are fortunately rare and nothing like as frequent as the lurid accounts of tiger-hunters have suggested. Even today in countries where the tiger has been given legal protection, many an innocent animal shot is declared to have been a man-eater merely as a means of circumventing the law.

After my first survey of the Sunderbans, a German scientist, Dr Hubert Hendrichs, spent several months there studying the problem of the man-eaters. He was able to ascertain that this behaviour was restricted to only part of the tiger population and that it was clearly related to those areas with the highest salinity. The remaining part of the population behaved 'normally', by avoiding contact with humans and showing no sign of inherent aggression. By examination of the carcasses of man-eaters which were shot, he deduced that their ferocity towards man arose from physiological damage to the liver and kidneys, from the constant ingestion of salt water. Fresh water sources are very limited in the Sunderbans. Although these conclusions await confirmation by further studies, it appears that a problem which has plagued scientists for many years may yet be overcome. If it is, it should be possible to devise a management plan for the Sunderbans in which the interests of man and the tiger can be equally safeguarded.

Apart from the man-eating tigers, there are other hazards in the Sunderbans. If one is hardy enough to wade ashore through the glue-like mud and the maze of sharp pneumatophores, one is faced by an almost impenetrable wall of tangled vegetation closely bound by strangling vines. With the aid of a machete one can hack a way through this, but woe betide the man who cannot retrace his footsteps: in such an enveloping jungle, exhaustion comes quickly from the heat and humidity. It is moreover the haunt of countless venomous snakes, which are very difficult to see. On the first occasion when one of the members of my party went ashore, he was confronted by a large cobra coiled among the branches at eye level. The forest guard who accompanied him was terrified, but my companion, as a good naturalist, had the courage to film the cobra before retreating.

Having enjoyed the experience of watching tigers in the wild in other countries, I was anxious if possible to see one of the famous Sunderbans tigers, whether man-eaters or not. There were numerous fresh pug-marks in many of the muddy creeks through which we passed, though there seemed little chance that we should see a tiger in daylight from a motor launch which inevitably advertised our approach in advance. With the help of the forest guards we therefore erected a *machan*, or tree-hide, on one of the few islands providing dry ground, in the hope of seeing one at night. There were fresh pug-marks on the shore and by a water-hole near the tree. To encourage the tiger, the guards tied a small sheep to a stake beneath the tree. As no trees in the Sunderbans are able to grow to any considerable height on account of the salinity, the *machan* platform was only twelve feet above ground, a height which the guards warned me could probably be reached without difficulty by any hungry tiger. Although I had never previously carried a weapon when watching tigers, I agreed to borrow a ·375 Magnum, a rifle capable of felling an elephant let alone a tiger, and hung this on a convenient branch as a precaution. Well camouflaged and with a powerful torch at my side, I then settled down at dusk for a long night's vigil.

The little sheep, unconcerned by fate, munched the sparse grass for a while and then, after scraping a comfortable hollow in the sandy ground, lay down and began to doze. As the sun sank behind the trees the chital deer began entering the clearing, their beautifully spotted coats shining sleekly in the fading light. A young buck, its three-tined antlers still in velvet, wandered towards the *machan* and was just in range of my camera when it caught sight of the sheep. Its head shot up and with a single spring-heeled bound it jumped twenty feet sideways and raced for cover. With the flash of its white tail, every chital in sight also instinctively ran a few paces. For ten minutes they stood alert, scenting the air with twitching noses, peering this way and that, and stamping nervously. Then, finding no danger, they resumed feeding.

A little later, a troupe of macaque monkeys passed noisily along the edge of the jungle, crashing about in the branches as though enjoying the commotion. Soon afterwards the first jungle cocks 'wound up' with a series of clucking notes and let fly with a strident crowing. Another and another answered and for a while I could hear them from every direction. Having completed their vespers, they fell silent. Then, as the last of the light faded, a big gecko lizard began calling a resonant '*gec-ko, gec-ko*' from the trees behind me. Cicadas were now strumming all over the clearing, sawing away with the notched ribs beneath their wing-cases to produce an astonishing volume of sound. Finally the jungle nightjars struck up their hollow, interminable knocking, like the sound of someone beating a wooden box with a stick.

I placed my now useless camera between my feet, tucked up my collar against the cold night air and concentrated my attention on the just discernible blob in the grass which marked the sleeping form of the sheep. I wished it would bleat to advertise its presence, but it remained staunchly silent. The chital had disappeared.

Two hours after sunset the nightjars and cicadas ceased singing and there followed a long period of complete silence, broken only by the occasional shrill bark or stamp of a distant chital, or by some other mysterious cry or disturbance in the jungle. One's imagination is sharpened to a high pitch in the velvet blackness of night in such a setting. I could imagine the thousand pitiless dramas which were being enacted in the darkness of the tangled trees, the hunter and the hunted twisting and turning among the clutching roots and vines, the hot blood spilling on the fetid mud. In the sunny light of day the face of the jungle wore an expression of guileless enchantment, where colourful butterflies, shining sunbirds, exquisite orchids and scented vine blossoms disguised the dark tragedies of the night.

I shook my head. This was just romantic anthropomorphism and I knew it. The orchids were mere parasites and the yellow and scarlet trumpets of the vines could not mask the fact that the plants were vicious stranglers, which killed their hosts as surely, if more slowly, than the tiger killed the defenceless chital, or the shikra hawk struck down the emerald dove. It was all part of the natural process of competition for survival.

Around midnight the dew began to fall and fat drops of

water dripped noiselessly from the waxy leaves above me, gently saturating my shoulders. It was now intensely cold and I was glad of the hot tea which I sipped cautiously from my thermos. The long night dragged on uneventfully, while I grew steadily colder and wetter. I was too busy with my thoughts to feel sleepy.

At four-thirty the sky began to pale in the east and a few minutes later the first black-headed orioles began to call their rich fluty notes. Within fifteen minutes the whole jungle was filled with bird voices and the scene changed swiftly from black and grey to gold and green. The drongos which had shared my tree while roosting shook the dew from their feathers and flew off towards the river. Flocks of parakeets wheeled overhead, screeching excitedly as they always do. Bee-eaters, laughing thrushes and various babblers joined the chorus to welcome the dawn and a brown-winged kingfisher gave out peal after peal of its strident laughter down by the hidden creek. The well-contented little sheep rose stiffly and shook its dew-soaked coat, sending a parabola of spray flying. I was happy that it had not been sacrificed, even though this meant that I had had neither sight nor sound of a tiger. As the first rays of the sun touched the trees, I got out my walkie-talkie set and asked for a launch to take me back to breakfast.

Although on this occasion the tiger had let me down, time spent in such a setting is never wasted and in a quiet way it had been a night to remember.

9 The Last of the Pachyderms

It had rained heavily all night. The noise of water dripping
from the trees on to the carpet of big leaves below was strangely
loud in the pre-dawn darkness. My wife and I climbed up the
wet backside of our kneeling elephant and settled ourselves
with legs astride the corner pillars of the sodden *howdah*,
which was merely a stuffed straw mattress with a wooden rail
around it. The elephant's front legs were ponderously straight-
ened up and then the back, with the deep pitching motion I
had come to know so well. The *mahout*, his head muffled in a
shawl against the cold, was lifted on the elephant's trunk to his
seat behind her ears and we were off at a steady rocking-chair
gait of nine-foot strides. In the first clearing, the sky was
brightening. Silhouetted on a dead tree, a white-backed vulture
shook the moisture from its shaggy plumage with a rattling
sound. The first gibbon began whooping somewhere in the
forest to our left. The jungle was awakening.

There is nothing to equal the excellence of watching wildlife
from the back of a well-trained elephant. To begin with, it
provides an uncannily silent form of transport. Other animals
are not alarmed by its approach. It affords a high vantage point
in thick jungle and ploughs through 20-foot elephant grass as
easily as a battleship through heavy sea. Deep swamps and
rivers are crossed without hesitation. At a word of command
an elephant will stand still, even if confronted by a tiger or a
rhinoceros. Finally, if one drops a lens hood or a lighter, the
elephant's trunk seeks it out unerringly in long grass and delicately hands it back to the *howdah*. Moreover, it is a self-
fuelling vehicle, which feeds as it goes.

In some African game reserves there are now too many

elephants for the limited land available to them. In consequence they are rapidly destroying the trees on which they depend for food and on which their small young are dependent for shade. In Asia, however, there are no really large reserves and the Indian elephant is dying out. The modern world has little room for large wild animals, particularly those which compete with human interests. The continuing reduction of Asia's once limitless forests, which were the home of the Indian elephant, and their replacement by agriculture, brings the animal into direct conflict with man. Farmers naturally object to herds destroying their crops. Trained elephants have greatly increased in value and are in constant demand for the logging camps, and this has created an additional pressure on the remaining wild population from which they are recruited. The traditional *khedda* method by which they are driven into stockades and shackled for training is severely criticized by conservationists, because of the disturbance it causes to such sensitive animals. Selective dart-gunning would be a more humanitarian method and would result in much less serious dispersal of the family groups. But there are now few large herds left. In regions such as the Chittagong Hill Tracts, where *kheddas* were once an annual tourist spectacle, they have had to be largely abandoned.

Our elephant was taking us into the Jaldapara Reserve in north Bengal, at the beginning of our tour of the last refuges of the Indian rhinoceroses. It is a small and scenically beautiful reserve of riverine forest and used to be a favourite target for poachers. No fewer than thirty of the now extremely rare rhinos had been killed there in the previous two years, in order that their horns could be sold as a supposed aphrodisiac. The guards, whose low wages made them easy prey to bribery, had recently been replaced by a larger and better disciplined force of new men. But access to the reserve was all too easy from the tongue of occupied village land which had been permitted to penetrate into the centre of the protected area. The chances of survival for the forty-five remaining rhinos looked rather slender.

By the time we reached the marshes, the sun had risen,

though rain was again falling. The elephant grass, arching over our heads, saturated us with water as we ploughed through it. In the occasional clearings and river beds, hog deer and big-antlered sambar were numerous. The rotund little hog deer, with their curiously egg-shaped bodies and low-hung heads, looked very defenceless in an area inhabited by tigers and leopards; yet here, as everywhere offering extensive marshes, they seemed able to maintain a high population density. We noticed rhino tracks and fresh droppings, and several times heard rhinos moving away in the high grass; but with good reason they were too shy to come into the open. Jaldapara is too small (only forty square miles) and too vulnerable to have great value as a sanctuary for endangered species. Nevertheless, in a country such as India, where land for wild animals is always threatened by the needs of the enormous human population, one has to be grateful for even the smallest reserve. It is simply unrealistic to think in terms of Kenya's magnificent 8,000-square-mile Tsavo National Park.

The following day we moved on to Assam, where two re-markable rediscoveries of animals thought to be extinct had recently occurred. One of these was the pygmy hog, the other the hispid hare. Both are miniature animals about which next to nothing was known when it was realized that it was too late to study them. Their rediscovery was the work of the Assam Valley Wildlife Society, which had been created by a group of British and Indian tea planters in the 1960s, thanks largely to the enthusiasm of Richard Magor. Both animals had been known to occur in small numbers until 1958 in the southern foothills of the Himalayas, most of which have now been extensively developed for agriculture, or as tea gardens. In 1971, however during the burning of a forest tract near a tea estate at Attaree-khat, it was reported that several very small pigs had been killed by the foresters. Richard Magor immediately gave orders that the killing should cease and that efforts should be made to catch one of the pigs for examination. A few days later, first a young male and then an adult female were caught. The latter, standing barely 12 inches high, had only three pairs of teats, instead of the six which occur in the wild boar, and was obviously an authentic pygmy hog. Several more were caught later and were successfully bred in captivity. In the same period a hispid hare was caught, but unfortunately did not survive. This curious little animal, often called the Assam rabbit, has remarkably small ears and short, stiff fur. I had seen what I believed to have been a hispid hare one evening in the Khasi-Jaintia hills in 1968, but thought the record so unlikely that I did not report it. It now seems that it was probably correctly identified.

Richard Magor sent his light plane to meet me at Gauhati while my wife went on by road to await me at Assam's famous Kaziranga National Park. During the morning I was able to land at the two tea estates where the captive pygmy hogs were being kept. It was an exciting experience to see a species which was thought to be extinct (*see* Plate 6). The little pigs were in fine fettle and, though extremely shy, looked happy enough in their enclosure. They ran with amazing speed on their disproportionately tiny feet. Unlike the wild boar, they have no tusks; speed is their only defence from the leopards and other cats which prey on them. A minute piglet bred in captivity was by contrast completely tame and permitted me to handle it and to feed it from a saucer. Its uniformly brown body had no trace of the characteristic striping of the young wild boar. One pair of adults had made a nest — a globular mass of grass, with entry and exit tunnels beneath it, well hidden among the stems of the 4-foot naul grass which had been transplanted from their wild habitat to the pen. Much of the credit for successfully rearing these ultra-rare animals in captivity goes to Mrs Robin Wrangham, whose husband manages the Paneery tea estate. The area where the pygmy hogs were found has now been put under protection.

Having inspected the site of this discovery, I flew on to rejoin my wife. Flying at low altitude over the great marshes of the Kaziranga, I was able to count twenty-six rhinoceroses, some with small calves; the population density seemed very high for such large and territorially-minded animals. They were easy to see, looking from the air like fat white mushrooms scattered over the vivid green marshes.

The Kaziranga is one of India's finest reserves and is well managed. Although of only 166 square miles, it contains the largest single remaining population of the great Indian rhinoceros in Asia. At the time of our visit there had been a good breeding season and the total had risen to 658. In the adjoining forests there were 400 elephants, 29 tigers and 300 barking deer. The rhinos shared the marshes with about 500 wild buffalo, a similar number of barasingha swamp deer and large numbers of hog deer and wild boar. In terms of numbers of visible animals, Kaziranga is the only reserve in India which approaches the spectacle offered by the great African reserves.

When the heat of the day had subsided, my wife and I rode into the swamps on a stately elephant and were able to see a considerable number of rhinos. The reserve manager told us that several of them had killed each other during territorial fighting and he shared my view that the population density was now too high for the available grazing. We heard two such combats in progress — a sudden thunder of heavy feet followed by the noise of an impact like a bus hitting a brick wall. When rhinos fight, the commotion and the noise are awe inspiring.

Out in the open areas of the marsh were herds of barasingha, placidly resting by the water's edge. The old stags had almost black coats and were magnificently antlered. Around each herd the snow-white cattle egrets were busily feeding, or were perched on the backs of the deer, looking for skin parasites. The buffaloes were more nervous of our approach, quickly gathering into defensive groups behind the massive bulls, which glared at us with raised heads and with their four-foot, back-swept horns along their shoulders. They, too, were closely attended by cattle egrets, many of which rode as passengers on their sleek backs.

Heading back into the sunset across the grassy margin of a lake, our elephant showed us a new trick. The ground was spongy. Each time she wrapped the tip of her trunk around a tussock of succulent grass to pull off a mouthful, the whole clump was uprooted, including several pounds of muddy soil. Without altering her steady stride, she neatly knocked the sod against the forward-swinging sharp edge of her fore-foot, scattering the soil before lifting the grass to her mouth. Like everything an elephant does, it was an impeccably executed and beautifully rhythmical action.

Entering the sea of elephant grass again, we came suddenly face to face with a rhino suckling her calf. Instantly she prepared to charge and the game warden reached for his rifle. Our elephant stopped, curled back her trunk and let out a deafening blast of trumpeting. The rhino hesitated, snorting angrily and taking short steps this way and that. She would not retreat, so we turned aside and circled past her at a respectful distance. You can't fool with a rhino with a small calf. The warden told us that a shot over-head did not always deter a rhino; but elephants were too valuable to risk having them gored. Our elephant knew all about rhinos and her shrill voice was respected.

As the sun went down in crimson glory, we watched flight after flight of pelicans, egrets and whistling teal passing in black silhouette against the afterglow. We had been riding for many hours and our elephant was tired after so much heavy going through the mud. When we came to the final stretch, which was of water up to her belly, she had obvious difficulty in dragging her legs out of the deep mud. I felt relieved for her when she clambered out on to the bund at the far side. We dismounted in complete darkness and were poled across the river in a leaking canoe to where our Land-Rover was waiting.

The following morning we had an opportunity to examine a rhino at closer quarters. We were out at dawn on another elephant in a heavy mist and came on a big male lying in a wallow. It clambered out laboriously on the far side. Our elephant moved forward slowly until we were only thirty feet apart. The rhino stared at us myopically with its tiny eyes, sniffing the air with flared nostrils. The wind was in our faces and carried our scent away. We gazed back at the huge creature, which was wet and black up to the water-line and white above with dry, caked mud from previous wallows.

The great Indian rhinoceros is a far more massively built animal than either of the African species (*see* Plate 7). An adult male weighs fully four tons, compared with the two-ton African black rhino, or the three to nearly four tons of the African white. Both African species have two often very long and slender horns; the Indian has a single short, broad horn. Its hide hangs in deeply folded, armour-like plates around the forequarters and rump, instead of the smoother, more hippo-like hide of the Africans. The skull is squat and snub-nosed. There are other, more curious differences. Neither of the Africans have incisor teeth, whereas the Indian has broad upper incisors and heavy, sharp-edged tusks in the lower jaw. Apart, perhaps, from the marine iguana of the Galápagos and the giant monitor lizard of Komodo, I know of no animal which so immediately brings to mind a prehistoric monster with a tiny brain. Studying the armour-plated colossus which stood swinging its head uneasily on the other side of the little pond, I felt something was missing. Of course — rivets! It resembled one of the early army tanks which had sheets of armour riveted to their flanks.

Our third rhino sanctuary was the Chitawan National Park, in Nepal, to which we flew a few days later. I had already visited this beautiful area in the lowland terai on previous occasions by light aircraft. The tourist brochures now spoke of a regular flight from Kathmandu by Royal Nepalese Airways; but because of the capricious nature of the weather for flying in Nepal, I knew it was wise to have a few days in hand. Sure enough, our plane was half a day late in taking off and two days late bringing us back from Chitawan. A heavy mist at Kathmandu caused the first delay. The second was due to our plane having been diverted for ministerial use elsewhere. We spent most of the two lost days riding back and forth by elephant from the reserve rest-house to the airstrip at Mghauli, or sitting for hours in the open-sided thatched shelter which represents the total amenities of the airport. There is no ground staff, just the shelter beside which the elephants wait patiently for an aircraft which may, or may not, arrive.

Our few days at Chitawan were nevertheless enjoyable. The sunlit marshes were full of game and the forests beyond alive with spectacular birds such as orioles, minivets, sunbirds, babblers and laughing thrushes. The 'Tiger Tops' rest-house,

5. We landed bumpily at 12,400 feet in an enclosed stony valley at the foot of Mount Langtang, near the Tibetan border. With the adjacent Gosainkund lakes, it would make a superb national park. *Below l. to r.*: The peaks of Nuptse, Everest, Lhotse and Ama Dablam, seen from the Khumjung lodge in the newly created Everest National Park.

6. A young pygmy hog, a species thought to be extinct but recently rediscovered. Thanks to the Assam Valley Wildlife Society, this unique little
animal is now being bred in captivity and the area where it occurs is protected.
Below: The rudimentary airport near Nepal's Chitawan Reserve, where
elephants wait patiently for a plane which may, or may not, arrive.

which had recently been taken over by Jim Edwards, has a superb setting on the bank of the river and provides a fine vantage point for watching the panorama of wildlife around it.

In spite of continuous poaching, the population of rhinos at Chitawan still exceeded 100 and we obtained photographs of some of them without difficulty. The reserve had been a problem to conservationists for many years. Although it is the most important wildlife sanctuary in Nepal because of its rhinos, which now survive nowhere else in the country, poaching has remained an intractable menace. Not only were rhinos being killed, but huge numbers of domestic cattle and illegal wood-cutters were destroying the grazing and forests. From a light aircraft flying at tree-top level, I have photographed streams of bullock carts crossing the Rapti River into the reserve. Under an old regulation, farmers were permitted to extract dead trees for fuel. In order to obtain 'dead' trees, they ring-barked living trees with axes and I counted dozens of such examples along the forest tracks. The reserve had a large number of armed guards, but instead of searching for poachers, many of them were sitting in their huts when we were there. Their wages were far too small to resist bribery from the poachers and the men lived in fear of being shot if they attempted to intervene. Happily this sorry situation has been taken in hand by the Nepalese Government since our last visit. A rhino and cattle-proof fence has been erected on the most vulnerable boundary and the protection of the area has been greatly strengthened. A large number of poachers have also been arrested.

The threat of extermination of the Asiatic rhinoceroses has now become imminent. The total number of surviving Indian rhinoceroses is today only about 800; the Sumatran species, which has a range extending to Burma, is now in the very low hundreds. The distinctive and smaller Javan rhino is even closer to extinction, with a total population of only forty-five. As with the African species, the threat to the survival of all three Asiatic rhinos rests on the single factor of the superstition that the ground-up horn, if taken orally, restores sexual virility in man. To kill a four-ton rhino merely in order to hack

7

off its horn, is like knocking down a cathedral in order to steal the cross on its spire. The carcass is normally left to rot; but if the poachers are undisturbed, they sometimes take the whole animal for sale. Even rhinoceros urine fetches a good price in India, as a 'cure' for asthma, and is sold by zoos.

In 1967 a Sumatran rhinoceros crossed the frontier near Cox's Bazaar, from Burma into Bangladesh, and was shot. Its carcass, cut into small pieces, earned the poachers the equivalent of £1,150 on the black market. The horn was sold at the rate of nearly £50 a pound. So long as this horrible trade persists, the rhinoceros is doomed. And for nothing more than an obviously fallacious superstition. At a dinner given in aid of the World Wildlife Fund in New York, the Duke of Edinburgh, referring to the mainly Chinese demand for rhino horn, stated that for all the good it could do as an aphrodisiac 'they might just as well grind up the leg of a kitchen chair'. He was quite right, but the remark led to a diplomatic protest, though China certainly represents the main source of income to the poachers throughout south-east Asia and Africa. Some Chinese peasants also believe that they can obtain either sexual virility or physical courage by consuming the flesh, blood, or ground-up bones of a tiger.

The general public of the world responds readily to the plea that beautiful or cuddly animals such as the giant panda or the koala should be preserved for posterity. The problem is more difficult when the survival of an 'ugly' animal such as a rhinoceros or a crocodile is involved. Yet these, too, are unique products of evolution and equally important representatives of the diversity of life on earth. The rhinoceros is part of our natural heritage. It does not compete with human needs. All it requires is the seclusion of the marshes and grass on which to graze. Surely we can protect a few such areas in order to preserve the last of the great pachyderms, if only to remind us that 150 million years ago their ancestors, the dinosaurs, dominated the small planet which we now dominate with such ruthless efficiency?

10 Monsoon Magic

On one of my visits to Burma during the War I was able to witness the beginning of the monsoon. It was late that year and in India the anxious farmers were already holding prayer meetings at the shrines of the Hindu god Varuna, the controller of the waters of life. For a week the sky had been darkened by towering thunderheads and in the parched plains the heat left one gasping for breath. Because of the extreme turbulence among the pre-monsoon clouds, my plane from Calcutta to the army base at Chabua, on the Burma border, was grounded. I therefore had to spend two days and a night in a succession of trains, changing periodically from broad to narrow-gauge tracks. The final stretch across forested Assam had been at snail's pace in a temperature of well over 100°F and I reached the tented camp near Chabua in a state of complete dehydration. The Medical Officer prescribed six pints of lime juice and water and as many salt tablets as an empty stomach would tolerate. I lay all night on my camp cot in a pool of sweat, listening to almost continuous thunder.

Next morning, feeling light-headed but well enough to resume my duties, I obtained a jeep and was driven to one of the battalion headquarters some thirty miles inside Burma. The narrow, dusty track led through magnificent tropical rainforest, in a series of steep switchbacks up and down the rounded hills, which rose to about 5,000 feet. White mist filled the valleys and lightning streaked constantly across the dark sky where clouds boiled like a witch's cauldron. The combination of extreme heat and high humidity was oppressive.

Nearing our destination, I noticed that the jeep engine was

overheating badly and told my driver to pull up at a stream and refill the radiator. He was a huge Kenyan from the King's African Rifles, whose front teeth had been filed into points, giving him a ferocious expression which belied his rather placid nature. Like most native drivers, he drove the jeep with a fearless disregard for survival. While he went off with his canvas bucket to fetch water, I smoked my pipe at the side of the road and watched some hornbills stripping the fruit from a wild fig. On a previous visit to Burma I had unwittingly eaten a hornbill, which had been served to me as 'chicken' by a Naga camp-cook; with heavily spiced rice it had been quite palatable. Ten minutes later my driver appeared, with a worried expression.

'Jeep go bang, Colonel Sir,' he said apologetically.

I had heard no explosion. However, a cloud of steam hung over the open bonnet of the jeep and a pool of black oil was spreading in the dust below it.

'Tell me what happened,' I said.

'Engine he very hot. I pour in water and he go bang,' he replied, rolling his eyes dramatically. I then noticed the oil filler cap lying on the cylinder head. He had poured half a gallon of water into the almost red-hot sump instead of the radiator. Not surprisingly, the sump had cracked.

'How long have you been a driver?' I asked. He grinned proudly, showing his imposing array of spiked teeth.

'I pass O.K. driver last week, Sir,' he replied.

Fortunately I was picked up by another passing jeep shortly afterwards and we towed in the crestfallen Kenyan.

Later that day I was talking to some officers in the command tent at the battalion camp when the monsoon broke. It came without warning — a sudden deafening roar of torrential rain on the canvas. We in Europe are accustomed to occasional heavy rain storms, which in our innocence we call 'cloudbursts'. Monsoon rain dwarfs such showers to insignificance. There is an explosive ferocity and a relentlessness about it which defies description. One cannot believe that such a volume of water has remained suspended in the clouds. It falls vertically, hitting the ground with such force that one feels it has been propelled, rather than obeying the mere laws of gravity. Within minutes the camp was awash and streams were boiling down the slopes, carrying with them a litter of debris and mud. Although the camp was sited on a hill-top, screened by trees, the ground everywhere became a morass and the jeeps which were racing to rescue bedding and equipment raised bow-waves of spray. Within a few hours the slit trenches of the guard-posts were full of water.

During the two weeks while I was in the region, the rain fell ceaselessly from an inky sky. It was impossible to dry either clothing or bedding. A tributary of the Chindwin River which snaked through the valley below, had risen by more than ten feet. Whole tracts of vegetation had begun to slide down the steeper parts of the hillside on the cushion of water which had collected between the subsoil and the bed-rock, leaving open scars on the ground. Part of the dirt road on which I had driven from Chabua had descended about six feet over a length of thirty yards and many big trees above the track had fallen across it as the soil was washed away from their roots. Engineers with bulldozers were working day and night to keep the vital road open. And only a few miles to the east of the camp, troops were having to fight the enemy in the incessant downpour. I cannot say I was sorry when I received orders to leave Burma and fly to Ceylon.

The region of northern Burma where the camp was located has an annual rainfall of 130 inches, compared with the average of twenty-nine inches enjoyed by England. In some parts of south-east Asia, where some rain falls during most of the year, the average exceeds 400 inches, the world record being held by Mount Waileale in Hawaii, which boasts an incredible average of 471·6 inches — almost forty feet of water in a year. Yet there are some parts of south-east Asia where the average is well below that of England. The controlling factor is the monsoon.

The word monsoon is derived from the Arabic *mausim* — a season. This seasonal continental wind system occurs twice a year over an area stretching from the Arabian Sea to China and southward to the northern parts of Australia. During the winter, the high plateau of central Asia beyond the Himalayas is very cold and forms a high pressure area away from which dry winds flow towards the equator. Here they meet winds flowing northwards away from high pressure over the Indian Ocean. As they cross the ocean, both southerly and northerly air-flows absorb moisture and carry it upwards as they meet. As the air cools, the moisture precipitates and falls as rain along the equator. The process is broadly speaking reversed in the summer, when the northern hemisphere receives the heat of the sun. The winds then flow north to fill the consequent depression, releasing the monsoon rain over India and south-east Asia. The summer monsoon continues in some regions for as long as five months of intermittent rain.

For reasons which are still obscure, the monsoon is subject to puzzling variations. Abnormal and disastrous rainfall occurs in some years, causing great losses; at other times large areas have no rain and then face famine. The monsoon moulds the whole face of Asia where its rains fall, smoothing off the shapes of mountains, carrying millions of tons of topsoil into the valleys and constantly re-shaping the courses of rivers. Countless towns and villages have disappeared during monsoon floods, only to be patiently rebuilt where they are equally liable to be swept away in subsequent years. But there are other, more powerful factors also at work. South-east Asia is geographically a very unstable area, where the earth's crust is still mobile, buckling under gigantic pressures. The Himalayas themselves are of comparatively very recent age, and they are still rising. In the Indonesian archipelagos a large number of volcanoes are very frequently active, and islands and the ocean floor are constantly changing their contours.

Since time immemorial the monsoon has been regarded in Asia as a blessing, bringing back life to the scorched land and water to dry wells. It governs men's whole lives and behaviour. Without it, large parts of Asia would be uninhabitable. Every year the arrival of the rains is celebrated with a fervour which repetition never diminishes. Memories of the disasters which follow a lack of rainfall are always too strong to blunt the spontaneous joy with which the first drops of life-giving water are received. Even the village buffaloes respond, bawling with pleasure as they head for the rapidly filling ponds, which for months have been cracked and sun-baked mud-holes; there they will lie ecstatically for hours with only their eyes and nostrils above the sweet blessing which falls from the sky.

The monsoon also completely regulates the behaviour of birds and vegetation. The migration and breeding of most bird species closely conforms to its arrival, so that advantage can be taken of the explosive abundance of insect life which follows. Many plants which provide fruit on which birds and other animals feed, bear fruit twice a year in conformity with the monsoon cycle. In different parts of Asia a variety of migratory bird species are regarded as the infallible heralds of the rain — the koel and other hawk-cuckoos, the rain-quail and the yellow wagtail are typical examples. Dr Dillon Ripley, who spent many years studying Asiatic birds, discovered a mountain tribe in Borneo which regulated its agriculture entirely by the bird calendar. When the yellow wagtails arrived from Siberia in September the rice was planted; seeding was done when a shrike from central Asia appeared in November; weeding when the sparrow hawks arrived from Japan in December; bundling when the migrant flocks of dusky thrushes swarmed in from Manchuria in January; harvesting awaited the first of the long-tailed munias, the notorious little seed-eating finches which devastate ripe rice crops. Though western farmers might smile at this, the accuracy of the movement of migratory birds in relation to weather and the abundance of food is not to be scoffed at.

The great rain forests of south-east Asia are products of the monsoon. Like those of South America and Africa, they occur only where the combination of high rainfall and constant high temperature is found. Though there is a similarity in the rain forests of all three continents in terms of the great height to which the trees grow and in their dense canopy interlaced with vines, the flora and fauna are, of course, very different. The Asian forests have been called the richest eco-system on earth. They have the greatest variety of different species; every new study produces long lists of additions new to science. Their variations in form are bewildering. There are trees such as the pandanus with stilt roots on which the base of the main trunk is raised high above the ground; trees with narrow, gracefully curved buttresses thirty feet high; trees which grow parasitically on other trees, dropping their own roots to the ground; trees such as the strangler fig, which climb by wrapping themselves like a gruesome web around their hosts until their weight kills them; trees which climb by hooking their barbed foliage into their hosts; trees such as the banyan which spread for fifty yards by dropping roots from their branches. Almost none are free from vines, ferns, orchids or other epiphytes which grow in rampant profusion in the moisture-saturated air. Some flower only once in fifteen years; others do so irregularly, branch by branch, while some of the *Ficus* species go on producing fruit throughout the year at two-monthly intervals.

The world's largest and most grotesque flowers occur here, such as the huge parasitic *Rafflesia* of Malaya and the repellent 'corpse flower' *Amorphophallus* of Sumatra, whose erect blossom can measure thirteen feet high by four wide. The diversity of species is illustrated by the example of a single volcano in the Philippines, which has a larger number of woody plant species than the whole of the United States. In Borneo there are 3,000 tree species, compared with about thirty native trees in Britain. A recent survey in the Malayan lowland forests showed that more than 200 tree species occurred in a sample plot of only five acres, whereas a similar sample in an old-established deciduous wood in Britain seldom exceeds nine or ten species.

In this world of tall trees, many animal species have evolved as expert climbers, long-jumpers, or gliders. There are giant flying squirrels which can glide for seventy yards on the extended membranes between their limbs and flying lizards which have membranes between their long, extensile ribs. The flying tree-frogs have membranes between their long toes. There is even a flying snake, the black and yellow paradise tree snake, which hurls itself from a branch and glides for fifty feet on the extended concave under-surface of its body. These forests also have the world's largest bats, the so-called flying foxes, or fox bats; they have a wing-span of five feet. The sight of their immense, evil-smelling colonies irrupting into flight in the evenings is spectacular. Fox bats feed on fruit and during their nightly journeys of up to twenty miles they contribute to the ecology of the forests by pollinating the flowers of mangos with the pollen which they accumulate on their heads while feeding. The interdependence of the life-forms of the rain forest and its sensitivity to the least disturbance is well illustrated by these bats. Some trees and other plants depend on a single species of bat, bird or insect to pollinate their flowers. The disappearance of any such species is therefore quickly reflected in the composition of the local flora.

The most successful gliding animal in the world lives in south-east Asia — the gentle colugo, a lemur-like creature which in flight resembles a square kite or a parachute as it glides from tree to tree on its four-foot-wide membranes. A glide of more than eighty yards has been recorded. Though so expert in climbing and gliding, the colugo is nearly helpless on the ground, where its huge membranes are a serious handicap.

Exploration in rain forests is difficult and arduous. Once inside, one can spend days without seeing the sky, except where a giant tree has fallen under the weight of its climbers. Such temporary clearings attract a profusion of foraging birds and butterflies. I have never been able to resist the temptation to linger in these welcome escapes from the prevailing gloom of the forests, where one longs for a breath of wholesome fresh air. Observation of the animal life is exceptionally difficult. There is movement everywhere, but one rarely gets more than a fleeting glimpse of something scuttling away. In the sunny leaf canopy perhaps two hundred feet above, there is a constant commotion of hidden parrots, hornbills, pigeons and monkeys enjoying the fruit. Only on the forest floor among the labyrinth of tangled roots, where there is little undergrowth because of the lack of light, can one actually examine the small creatures which are everywhere moving about in the deep, wet litter.

The variety of insect and reptile life inside the rain forests is beyond imagination. Almost everything one sees is new and different and frequently grotesque in form or dimensions. There are brightly coloured cicadas as large as mice, moths and butterflies of enormous size and breath-taking beauty, spiders with hard-shelled bodies and long horns, huge, poisonous centipedes, frogs with horns and incredibly loud voices, mantises in every conceivable form and colour, some of which closely resemble the orchids on which they await their prey. When Alfred Russel Wallace was collecting in Borneo in 1854, he identified from a single square mile of forest nearly 2,000 different species of beetles. Even bearing in mind that five-sixths of all the species of creatures inhabiting the world are insects, this is an astonishing figure. Many of the beetles of the rain forest are not only of grotesque form but of brilliant metallic colours and are worn as ornaments by the native tribes. Some are very large and extremely powerful creatures, notably the big rhinoceros beetles. I caught one of these and put it in a tobacco tin, only to find that within a minute it had forced off the lid. When I tried to hold it by the thorax, it easily forced my fingers apart and escaped.

Apart from the ever-present leeches and ticks, some of the rain forest insects are constant pests to man and wild animals alike — particularly the ants, termites, sweat-bees and biting flies. I suffered a fever and considerable pain from bites which were diagnosed as those of a jute moth. Probably the insect most feared is the so-called tiger hornet, which has a wing-span of three and a half inches. It is all too easy to stumble on one of their colonies in the litter of the forest floor, though they are fortunately not common. Half a dozen stings from these monsters are said to be sufficient to kill a man.

City-bred people, faced for the first time with the rain forest of south-east Asia, have described it as having a menacing or nightmare quality. Some of the soldiers who fought in the Burma campaign told me they were more afraid of getting lost in the forest than they were of the enemy. This is understandable when one considers the combination of impenetrability, oppressive atmosphere, relentless monsoon rain and the pullulating abundance of insect and reptile life. Add to this the strangling, hook-thorned vines, the huge, evil-smelling fungi and the almost unbelievable gigantism of the vegetation and one has the makings of a nightmare. Man's intrusion, at best, is furtive. But as object lessons in evolution and the diversity of nature, the rain forests are of unparalleled interest.

Most of the large wild animals of Africa are now familiar to millions of tourists; but those of the monsoon region of south-east Asia are for the most part unknown to the western world. How many people can call to mind the appearance of a banteng, a serow, a goral, or a takin? Yet these are just as fascinating as the better known wild oxen or wild goats of other regions. Two of the miniature animals certainly deserve world renown — the delightful little mouse-deer of the Malayan and Indonesian rain forests, which stands only ten inches high, and the world's smallest buffalo, the anoa of the Celebes Islands, which is a bare three feet high. There are many other curiosities, such as the armoured pangolin which walks on its knuckles, the comical proboscis monkey, the long-limbed gibbons which move through the tree-tops with such superb grace and agility, and the crimson and orange painted bats — the world's most colourful mammals. To this list one could add the clouded leopard, which is the nearest living relative of the sabre-toothed tiger, the woolly, prehensile-tailed binturong, the primitive four-toed tapir, and the highly intelligent orang-utan of Sumatra and Borneo, which zoo collectors have now nearly exterminated. Are there any animals more delightful or more curious than the slow loris, which creeps with such stealthy deliberation and wears such a forlorn expression, and the tarsier, which has the largest eyes of all the world's 193 primates? One could extend the old quip that a camel must have been designed by a committee and say that a tarsier looks as if it had been created by the world's leading cartoonists. Its enormous, immobile golden eyes occupy three-quarters of its tiny face. Its projecting ears are paper-thin and bat-like. The fingers on its hands are grotesquely long, like the legs of a spider, terminating in adhesive pads. Its hind limbs are disproportionately long, enabling it to jump like a furry frog. Its plump little six-inch body is covered with fine, silky fur and it has a ten-inch naked tail with a tuft at the tip.

The dominant animal is, of course, the tiger, of which four races or subspecies occur in south-east Asia. The Indian race, the so-called Bengal tiger, extends to the west of the Irrawaddy River in Burma. The Indo-Chinese tiger occupies a huge area from southern China to Malaya. Sumatra and Java each have their own distinctive races. There used to be another race in Bali, but this has recently been exterminated. Only about five Javan tigers are left. Everywhere this wonderful species is vanishing because of the ever-increasing exploitation of forests and excessive hunting, trapping and poisoning. All the wildlife of the forests is similarly threatened. It is a sombre reflection on man's destructive genius that, in a part of the world which is so little known, there are already no fewer than ninety species of mammals alone which are now nearing extinction.

The life-giving monsoon, whose annual magical transformation of the living world of south-east Asia makes possible its extraordinary diversity, has in the past restricted human interference. Primitive man conformed gratefully to these restrictions. His farming methods, which are still practised by the jungle tribes, were on a labour-intensive and diversified rotational basis, taking full advantage of both climate and soil. The small plots which he cultivated around his villages did little harm to the environment, because he returned all vegetable and animal waste to the soil and seldom stayed for long in the same place. Modern mechanized cereal farming, by contrast, exposes the soil for long periods to baking, leaching and erosion. The water-holding capacity and the plant nutrients of the soil quickly decline. The balance of insect life which the diversity of the forest provides, in which no one species can dominate, is destroyed. The populations of pest species are then free to explode in the extensive monocultures of crops. The mosquitos and other disease-vectors which here are normally restricted to the high tree-tops, swarm down into the clearing, bringing malaria and yellow fever to the farmer. After the first few harvests have been taken, the declining fertility of the land obliges the farmer to abandon it to grazing; but it is soon too poor even to support cattle. The cattle then have to feed in the adjoining forest, thus increasing the area of destruction. Finally the farmer gives up the farm and clear-fells a new tract of forest and repeats the process elsewhere, leaving behind him an exhausted land and a destroyed biotic community.

The giant rain forests cannot withstand the modern chainsaw or the bulldozer. As the rice and maize fields and the monocultures of rubber, teak or bananas expand, so the wonderful storehouse of evolutionary diversity declines. One by one the unique animals and strange plants which fascinated Marco Polo and Alfred Russel Wallace are disappearing for ever.

11 *The African Spectacle*

At a simple ceremony in Nairobi on the 29th of August 1973 H.R.H. Prince Bernhard, President of the World Wildlife Fund, handed to President Jomo Kenyatta a cheque for the equivalent of £210,000. It was the culmination of one of the great success stories in Africa's conservation history. The money given by the W.W.F. not only assured the future of the Lake Nakuru National Park, but increased the protected area from 14,261 to 42,549 acres.

The famous American naturalist Roger Tory Peterson, in whose company I have travelled in four continents, once described Nakuru as providing the greatest ornithological spectacle on earth. I agree with him. There is nothing to compare with the almost overwhelming sight of the lake when a million flamingos and tens of thousands of pelicans, ducks, cormorants and other aquatic birds are feeding there (*see* Plate 8). Its scientific, recreational and touristic values had long been recognized by the Kenyan Government, which gave it national park status soon after independence. Recently, however, the big estates surrounding it were being broken up and taken over for small-scale settlements and subsistence agriculture. The protective buffer zone around the park was threatened. At the same time the nearby town of Nakuru was expanding and officials wanted to discharge its sewage into the lake; this would inevitably have caused serious if not fatal pollution and destroyed the delicately balanced ecology of the reserve. The further extension of the park boundaries made possible by the donation from the W.W.F. removed the first threat and strengthened the hand of the government in preventing the second.

I first saw Nakuru in the company of Jack Hopcraft, a Kenyan citizen who, with his son John, has played a leading part in developing the protection of the lake and its surroundings. My wife and I were on holiday and I was enjoying the opportunity to relax instead of having to follow the strenuous routine of my more serious expeditions, which usually involved two months of intensive field work, followed by endless meetings with government officials. Expeditions meant leaving camp before or just after sunrise and by the time the daily log of observations had been completed the following evening it was eleven o'clock. Now I was keeping civilized hours and following a tourist routine, even though in every reserve we visited I was soon involved with the local conservation problems. We had a picnic lunch under a fever tree on the lake shore while we watched the ever-changing mass of birds which paddled, swam or flew like an animated carpet on and around the water. Just behind us in an adjacent tree a handsome augur buzzard with a snow-white breast was also lunching, showering the ground with the plumage of a coot which it held in its talons. To our right a marabou stork, the ghoulish scavenger of Africa, was deliberately stalking a young flamingo with a broken wing. The flamingo was watching the approach of its lugubriously bald-headed executioner with a kind of helpless fascination. Sooner or later it would die from a sword-thrust by that cavernous bill which the marabou kept half hidden against its flabbily dangling neck-pouch. Nothing comes amiss to the appetite of a marabou, be it offal, mammal, bird, fish or reptile, dead or alive.

To our left on a picturesquely gnarled dead tree overhanging the water sat three motionless darters. They were artistically posed with wings outspread and snake-like necks gracefully curved, drying their plumage after a diving session. Not even the most skilful Japanese artist could have posed them more decoratively. At the edge of the water, blacksmith and spur-wing plovers, spoonbills, sacred ibises, avocets and dazzling white little egrets darted this way and that on the warm mud.

And all around us the chorus of honking and gabbling of count-less flamingos filled the air.

With my binoculars I began cataloguing the birds visible from where we sat. I counted no fewer than twelve species of ducks, thirteen species of herons, egrets and storks and twenty different small waders. But of course I was merely skimming the surface. About 400 bird species and seventy different mammals have been recorded in the national park.

After lunch Jack drove us to the far end of the lake and out on to a long spit projecting into the water. Here we were able to sit in the centre of a group of perhaps ten thousand greater and lesser flamingos, which soon paid no attention to our immobile vehicle. From a distance of barely twenty paces we could see the rapid pulsations of their throats as they swung their hanging heads from side to side in the shallow alkaline water, pumping it through the comb-like lamellae inside their grotesquely shaped crimson and black bills to extract the blue-green algae, insect larvae and shrimps on which they fed. The Nakuru flamingos consume 180 tons of aquatic organisms every day. We had seen a few thousand flamingos on Lake Naivasha, farther down the Rift Valley, and I had studied them in the great Camargue and Coto Doñana Reserves in France and Spain, as well as in Asia; but never before had I seen them in such enormous numbers, nor so remarkably tame. Flamingos are normally very nervous birds. Perhaps at Nakuru their very numbers gave them a new self confidence.

Out of nowhere, with typical African suddenness, a storm came sweeping over the lake, blotting out the sun. At the first peal of thunder the birds around us rose, honking excitedly, in a dramatic blaze of crimson, black and white against the dark sky. For a while we were the centre of a blizzard of beating wings, dangling legs and outstretched necks. The flock settled again farther down the lake, gliding down on short, bowed wings and with angular legs trotting the last few yards. As the wings were folded, hiding the crimson, the flock changed magically to white.

Much of the money for the extension of Nakuru was raised by European children, who everywhere are now working

7. The now rare Indian rhinoceros has a single massive horn and a heavy, characteristically folded hide. Like the two smooth-skinned, twin-horned African species, it is constantly persecuted by poachers, who can sell the ground-up horn for more than its weight in gold as a supposed aphrodisiac. *Below*: A pair of African black rhinoceroses.

8.

Above: When a million flamingos are feeding on Lake Nakuru they provide the greatest ornithological spectacle on earth.

Left: From horizon to horizon long wavering columns of wildebeests migrate annually across the Serengeti plain.

enthusiastically to help the World Wildlife Fund. In February 1973 twenty-six prize winners among those who took part in the Nakuru campaign in Belgium, Germany, Great Britain, Luxembourg, the Netherlands, Sweden and Switzerland were taken on a two-week African safari. This included camping in the Amboseli Reserve, visiting the great Tsavo National Park and, of course, seeing Nakuru. A delightful little ceremony took place on the shore of the lake when Professor Mohamed Hyder and Mr Perez Olindo, respectively Chairman and Director of the Kenya National Parks, met and thanked the children. At another ceremony at the thriving wild animal orphanage at the gates of the Nairobi National Park, which children have also supported, Kenya's Minister for Tourism, the Hon. Jaxton Shako, unveiled a bronze statue of a Kenyan boy and a European girl holding hands across the back of a Grant's gazelle. A commemorative plaque on the plinth bears the panda symbol of the W.W.F. and pays tribute to the help provided by European children for the orphanage, which every year is visited by hundreds of parties of Kenyan school-children. The value of projects such as these is incalculable in terms of international good will.

Hundreds of thousands of children in Europe, Asia and Africa and also the Boy Scouts of the world are now helping the W.W.F. and learning about conservation through its activities. Many are doing practical and valuable work on local projects. Such actual participation, instead of just listen-ing to the complaints of their elders about the growing degra-dation of the environment, has a great appeal to young people. In Great Britain alone, inspired by the leadership of Cyril Littlewood, the Wildlife Youth Service has 240,000 members and the active support of 4,500 schools. By their own efforts, applied with great imagination and an astonishing variety of methods, these children had by 1973 raised about £100,000 in support of W.W.F. projects at home or abroad, in addition to cleaning up village ponds, planting trees, picking up litter, conducting animal censuses and a host of other useful tasks. The Conservation Corps, which now has links with the W.W.F., provides an outlet for the interests of older teenagers and

8

young men and women who wish to contribute to the practical aspects of conservation in Britain. People who complain about the attitudes of the youth of today should remember that the idealism of young people which so often leads to destructive protest can also lead to most valuable voluntary work, if it is given a worthwhile opportunity to express itself.

The three neighbouring countries of Kenya, Tanzania and Uganda have no fewer than sixty national parks and game reserves. All are different and all are worth seeing, either for the great variety and numbers of animals within them, or for the very rare species which some contain, or for the superb and differing scenery which they protect. The distinction between a national park and a game reserve in Africa is a bit tenuous. Broadly speaking a national park is intended to provide complete protection to all fauna and flora and no human utilization of the land is permitted. In a reserve, while all wildlife is protected and given priority, limited human activities such as cattle grazing are permitted. The distinctions vary somewhat, however, from country to country and in spite of efforts to obtain fixed standards of definition throughout the world, these have not yet been achieved.

Visiting African wildlife reserves can be either the experience of a lifetime or an exhausting and confusing marathon, according to whether one is well advised or merely accepts a typical package tour which offers visits to the maximum number of reserves in the shortest possible time. At the peak of the tourist season many of the most easily accessible reserves are now overcrowded with vehicles. Road travel between them, which is usually conducted by tour operators at high speed in order to save time, can be hot, dusty and uncomfortable. It is infinitely better to spend four or five days in each of, say, three reserves and to travel between them by the light aircraft services which are available, than to spend one day in each of six or seven reserves and an equal time in road travel, which is the pattern of most package tours. One then returns home refreshed and enriched instead of exhausted and confused.

If I had to initiate a friend to the spectacle of African wildlife, I would take him first to the Murchison Falls National

Park in Uganda. We would start from the Paraa Lodge, near the confluence of the Victoria and Albert Niles as they spill into Lake Albert. There used to be an elephant living near the lodge which amused itself by turning over parked cars at night; unfortunately it had to be shot after doing so when four German tourists were in a car which it capsized, so the lodge is peaceful again. We would then go by motor-launch up the Victoria Nile to the foot of the falls. This brief seven-mile journey is one of the most dramatic which one is ever likely to make. The river is not very wide and on both banks there is a constantly changing panorama of elephants, buffaloes, Jackson's hartebeests, Uganda kobs, oribis, waterbucks, Rothschild's giraffes and other animals peacefully going about their daily business. Both the black and the white rhinoceroses can be seen. The white (which is not really white but derived its name from the Dutch *weit*, meaning 'wide', in reference to its square muzzle) was almost wiped out in Africa by poachers. In the safety of Ugandan reserves and thanks to the efforts of the W.W.F. and the courage of the game wardens in catching poachers, it was saved in the nick of time. It is now multiplying so well that surplus animals have been moved into reserves in other parts of Africa.

Not only the banks of the Victoria Nile, but the river itself is rich in animal life. Hippopotamuses are numerous and from the launch can be seen at very close quarters. Some, torpid and immobile, doze on the sunny sandbanks; others lie submerged, with only their ears, eyes and nostrils above water. There is something rather endearing about hippos, with their sleek, barrel-shaped bodies, stumpy legs and enormous heads with tiny eyes set in pink eye-patches. What do they think about as they lie hour after hour, motionless in the river, or in their evil-smelling mud wallows, while little egrets, darters and even big goliath herons and whale-headed storks treat them as islands and perch casually on their backs? Though they look so placid, they can be dangerous to small boats when they have calves and their frequently gashed hides show how they can use their immense teeth when fighting.

Some of the largest crocodiles in Africa inhabit this stretch of the river and they are easily seen, lying on the banks with jaws a-gape, or sliding silently into the water as the launch approaches. Their colours and markings vary greatly. In many parts of Africa the skin-traders have completely exterminated crocodiles and even in the Murchison Park poachers are often at work. Unhappily, though crocodiles breed freely along the river, they lose most of their eggs to the big monitors which dig them up and eat them, or lose their newly emerged young to the ever-watchful marabou storks.

If my imaginary friend is interested in birds and if he is carrying John Williams's admirable *Field Guide to the Birds of East Africa*, he will be able to identify at least fifty different species during the short boat-ride, including some of the most beautiful of the kingfishers and bee-eaters. But the climax of the trip comes when the falls are sighted at the head of the gorge. The launch edges forward cautiously, as near as the powerful whirlpools permit. Flying spray and the thunder of millions of tons of water crashing through the narrow cleft in the rocks above fill the air. It is a spectacle to silence even the most talkative of sightseers.

The following day I would take my friend by road above the falls and let him walk the short distance to where he can look down on the river as it bursts through the crack in the gorge and falls vertically into the boiling cauldron below. When the sun is shining, a rainbow spans the spray-filled gorge. Hundreds of thousands of tourists have stood spellbound at this spot, their senses numbed by the noise and commotion. There is a terrible, mesmeric fascination about standing close to the crest of a big waterfall. On one side the racing water is oil-smooth; on the other, as it rockets into space, all is thunderous chaos. One cannot be surprised that the Murchison Falls have claimed their quota of suicides and accidents. Ernest Hemingway and his wife, trying unwisely to get a closer view of the falls from a light aircraft, crashed into the river and were miraculously rescued by a launch which happened to be near enough to save them.

The falls were first discovered in 1864 by the explorer Samuel Baker and his courageous wife. Mrs Baker walked across Africa in long Victorian skirts during their search for the source of the Nile. The national park has become a major source of tourist revenue to Uganda. The falls were, however, recently the focus of one of the hardest fought battles between 'developers' and conservationists. It was proposed to build a giant dam across the river and to reduce the spectacular falls to a mere trickle neatly channelled through a concrete pipe. Uganda could then obtain not only all the hydro-electric power it needed, but would have an immense surplus which could be sold profitably to neighbouring countries. This glowing prospect, as described by the enthusiastic civil engineers, seemed irresistible, especially as the cost of construction would probably be available from the World Bank. The battle for the preservation of the Murchison Falls National Park then began, with the World Wildlife Fund playing a leading role. Protests flowed in from all over the world; but battles of this magnitude cannot be won by indignation or emotional appeals. Careful research was conducted, including engineering feasibility studies of possible alternative sites for the dam.

When the facts had been marshalled, it was shown that the construction of the dam in the site proposed would involve several years of work by a very large labour force and that the approach road and hutments for labour and equipment, let alone the dam itself, would completely destroy the national park. The loss of the steadily growing revenue from tourism which the park attracted was shown to represent a major potential blow to Uganda's economy. Even though it might be recuperated by the income from surplus energy which the dam might provide, this revenue could be retained intact if the dam were built elsewhere. Finally, three perfectly satisfactory alternative sites, which would not damage the park, were available. Though the power these could produce would be less than from the original proposal, Uganda could still obtain far more than it needed in the foreseeable future. Finally, after more than a year of patient negotiation, reason prevailed and the Ugandan Government decided to retain the Murchison Falls and the national park intact for the enjoyment of the world.

The second place to which I would take my imaginary friend would be very different. We would stay at the beautiful Crater Lodge, 8,000 feet above sea level on the rim of the caldera of Ngorongoro in Tanzania. Here from the terrace, when the valley clouds have lifted, one can see the whole floor of the extinct volcano, which is nine miles wide. With binoculars, elephants and rhinoceroses can be seen moving about on the tawny plain. This is only the centre of the 2,500-square mile Ngorongoro Conservation Area. Originally it formed part of the adjacent Serengeti National Park, but has now the dual purpose of protecting wildlife while at the same time safeguarding the interests of the indigenous Masai, whose cattle are permitted to graze within the crater. Although not an ideal arrangement, because the cattle compete for the grazing with the wild ungulates and because it is difficult to prevent the Masai from continuing to prove their manhood by spearing occasional rhinos or lions, it avoids the accusation of depriving them of tribal lands.

From the lodge one enters the plain by the very steep and twisting Lerai Descent, 2,000 feet down the inside wall of the caldera. Only a vehicle with four-wheel drive and good brakes can safely negotiate this track. Arriving at the bottom, one drives at will into the grassy plain, which is dotted with marshy pools and patches of acacias and euphorbias. There are few better places for wildlife photography. Everywhere there are animals peacefully grazing, or, especially at dawn or dusk, hunting or being hunted.

Tourists in a hurry to see as many animals as possible in a short visit, zig-zag all over a reserve, stopping only momentarily to take pictures. This not only causes unnecessary disturbance, but deprives them of the opportunity of witnessing the many dramas which occur when animals are not preoccupied by watching tourists. It is far better to sit quietly in the vehicle at a likely spot, such as under a shady tree or near a waterhole, and let the animals come to you. Remarkably little attention is paid to a stationary car so long as the occupants are quiet and make no sudden movements. Animals in the African reserves have learned that vehicles do not threaten them. Only when

tourists are silly enough to disobey regulations and get out of
their cars do accidents occur. Some tourists, beguiled by the
tameness of the animals, act with incredible stupidity. A
German who was a keen camper ignored the advice of a
warden and pitched his tent in a site of his own choosing.
During the night he was killed and eaten by a lion. But the
disregard of animals for stationary vehicles can be very rewarding. On one occasion when my wife and I were watching
a leopard which had just killed a waterbuck, it dragged the
carcass right up to the shade provided by our Land-Rover
before beginning its meal. On another occasion, when we had
parked beneath a big tree, a lioness which was taking a siesta
in it, presently moved out along a branch above us and subsided with a sleepy yawn and with the tip of her tail hanging
within a foot of the open roof of the car. Such moments can
rarely be enjoyed by a chattering group which is for ever
hurrying to see the next 'new' animal.

There are lions galore in the Ngorongoro. At the height of
day they are lethargic and one is fortunate to see them doing
anything except lolling about in the sun, or digesting their food
in sprawling groups under a tree. But at first light or at sunset
there is a chance that from a good vantage point one can be
rewarded by seeing the whole sequence of a hunt, from the
selection of the intended victim and the careful positioning of
the pride to intercept its escape, to the usually inevitable kill.
Cheetahs, too, inhabit the crater, though they are not numerous. The flat open plain is an ideal place to watch them hunting. A walking cheetah looks a rather ungainly animal. One
could be forgiven for thinking it deformed by comparison with
a leopard. Its head looks too small, its legs too thin and its
long, sagging back is unlike that of any other member of the
cat family. But whereas a leopard hunts by stalking and
pouncing, or by dropping on its prey from a tree, a cheetah is
a chaser and built for maximum speed and agility in turning
at full gallop. Even the fastest gazelle can rarely escape once
a cheetah begins its final 60-miles-an-hour dash; no matter
how quickly it twists and turns, the cheetah follows every

move with split-second accuracy. The final chase is usually very brief.

The number of different species of animals which can be seen in the Ngorongoro crater is astonishingly large for an enclosed area of only 102 square miles. Obviously some of them move in or out by climbing the surrounding rim, though in places this rises to nearly 11,000 feet above sea level. Apart from the commoner species such as zebras and various antelopes, there are some fine herds of the world's largest antelopes — the corkscrew-horned elands — and some well-marked Masai giraffes, which, unlike the related common and Rothschild's giraffes, have sharply jagged edges to the pattern of markings on their bodies. Spotted hyenas are very common here and it is a good place to see the delightful little black-faced bat-eared foxes and large parties of varicoloured hunting dogs. Around the rocky rim of the crater there are olive baboons and in the forested parts, if one is lucky, it is possible to see the giant forest hog, a huge, mainly nocturnal pig with powerful tusks and monstrously swollen, crescentic, wart-like growths below its eyes; this unprepossessing creature was first discovered for science by my redoubtable old friend, Colonel Dick Meinertzhagen in 1904.

For the third and last reserve to be seen by my friend on his first visit to Africa (for three would be sufficient if he is to do justice to them in two weeks at a leisurely pace), I would choose the Serengeti National Park. This is often called 'the great African spectacular' and it certainly provides the greatest opportunity to see game animals in enormous numbers. Scenically its 5,600 square miles are a delight. The huge central plain is relieved by high granite *kopjes* of noble proportions and there are attractive areas of savanna and woodlands, as well as occasional small lakes. The Grometi, Orangi, Bologonja and Mbalageti Rivers, which run from east to west through the park, are well forested.

Serengeti is only a short drive from Ngorongoro and we would have planned our trip so that its climax might coincide with the great migration of the wildebeests, which normally occurs in May or June. Seen from ground level it is an unforgettable spectacle. From a light aircraft, which was the way I first saw it, it is almost unbelievable. From horizon to horizon, marching often eight or ten abreast, four or five parallel wavering columns of wildebeests head westward across the plain (*see* Plate 8). Many zebras, impalas, topis and gazelles march with them. When the winter rains have restored the burnt-out plain to vivid green, they will return. On either side of the columns, numerous lions, hyenas, jackals and hunting dogs watch hungrily, ready to cut out any straggler or weakling which falls behind. Year after year this tremendous animal pilgrimage to new pastures is repeated. When they cross the roads in the reserve, cars have to wait until there is a momentary gap before slipping through. Sometimes calves are dropped during the migration and one can only watch helplessly as the hunting dogs close in and, despite the courageous efforts of the mothers to keep them at bay, quickly tear them to pieces. It looks horribly cruel, but it is part of the natural pattern of life of both species and the effect on the survival of the wildebeest population is infinitesimal.

The Serengeti has one of the longest bird-lists of any park in East Africa. About 450 species have been recorded there. These include no fewer than thirty-five different birds of prey, ranging from the fierce little finch-size pygmy falcon to the great martial eagle. The Masai ostrich and six species of bustards can be seen on the plains. I thought I had made a very fine list of birds there until Myles Turner, the chief game warden, took me out in his Land-Rover. He is one of the best ornithologists in Africa and before we returned he had shown me nearly fifty species which I had missed. Among them was the magnificent Schalow's turaco, a big bird with an emerald green body, scarlet wings and a long crest.

In the evening, while we were drinking sundowners on the terrace of the Seronera Lodge, which is in the centre of the national park, Myles talked about his job. To most people, the life of a game warden in such a superb area sounds idyllic and full of romance. In fact, it is an arduous life, a combination of bureaucratic frustration, ceaseless cross-country travel by Land-Rover, light aircraft or on foot, fighting bush fires or drought, and no little danger in apprehending poachers who do not hesitate to defend themselves with guns or poisoned arrows. It is not only a miserably paid job in relation to the responsibilities involved, but one without security for the future. Only a deep love of the wilds and a sense of dedication to the protection of wildlife keeps such men at their posts year after year. I have met them in many different countries. They are the unsung heroes of conservation and without their skill and devotion the wildlife reserves of the world would be ineffective.

I would want my imaginary friend to spend the last evening of his tour in the company of such a man. We would watch the sun go down in one of the glorious, flaming sunsets which Africa nearly always provides. As the light faded, we would listen to the gradually rising diapason of the wildlife at night, the owls, the nightjars and the frogs, the shrilling of millions of cicadas and crickets, the insane, wailing laughter of the hyenas and the barking, grunting, shrieking and whinnying of countless other animals feeding or prowling in the darkness. By day, even in the incandescent blaze of high noon, the wilds of Africa provide an ever-changing spectacle; by night they are never completely silent.

12 Darwin's Treasure Islands

There are three sea-routes by which the Galápagos Islands can be approached — south-west from Panama, which is about 1,000 miles; north-west from Lima, about 1,200 miles; or due west along the equator for 600 miles from Guayaquil in Ecuador. On different occasions I have used all three during my five visits to the archipelago. But from whichever direction one approaches, the first sight of the islands provides a similarly dramatic impact. Not only do they look unlike any other islands one has ever seen, but it is impossible to behold them without an anticipatory thrill of excitement, or without recalling the profound effect which they have had on human thought during the past century. The Galápagos were, in fact, the birthplace of evolutionary biology and, as such, are still regarded as the world's most important living laboratory for the study of the evolutionary process.

Charles Darwin was only twenty-two years of age when he signed on as naturalist aboard H.M.S. *Beagle* in 1831. His ship was 90 feet long and weighed only 242 tons; nevertheless it was regarded in those days as 'suitable' for a five-year voyage around the world. Diffident, but almost unbelievably industrious in spite of constant seasickness, Darwin was soon held in high esteem by Captain Fitzroy, who, himself little older, thought him 'a very superior young man and the very best that could have been detailed for the task'. There was no aspect of natural history to which Darwin did not apply his ever-enquiring mind and, as the long voyage progressed, the number of his bulging notebooks and crates of specimens steadily increased.

Having rounded the southern tip of South America in 1835, the *Beagle* sailed north along the Pacific coast, making a final call at Callao before heading north-west to the then almost unknown Galápagos. Both Darwin and Fitzroy were appalled by their first impression of the black volcanic islands. Darwin described them as 'a country compared to what we might imagine the cultivated parts of the infernal regions to be'. Fitzroy's comment was more succinct: 'a fit scene for pandemonium'.

Galápago is the Spanish word for tortoise. Since the very first visits of the buccaneers and pirates, the islands were chiefly known for the giant tortoises which could so easily be collected and stored alive on board, as a welcome change from the weevil-infested salt pork with which ships were normally provisioned. But though this food source was plentiful, fresh water was extremely scarce and is even today available on only three of the islands. The first discoverer of the Galápagos, Fray Tomas de Berlanga, Bishop of Panama, found none and was reduced to chewing cactus to quench his thirst. Writing of this experience in 1535, he described the islands as 'looking as though God had caused it to rain stones'. The buccaneer Woodes Rogers, who had just rescued Alexander Selkirk (the original Robinson Crusoe) from Juan Fernandez Island, called the Galápagos 'nothing but loose rocks, like cinders — not the least sign of water, nor is it possible that any can be contained on such a surface'.

The islands are the exposed tips of submarine volcanoes, which erupted about one million years ago, two miles beneath the surface of the Pacific. A few are still active and thirty-five eruptions have been recorded in the past 160 years. When my wife and I were having supper with some friends on the beach of Isabela Island on the 21st of May 1968, we had the unusual experience of witnessing the birth of a violent eruption on the opposite island of Fernandina. A number of high jets of molten lava suddenly spouted from the flank of the 4,500-foot caldera and began flowing down the slope. When our ship left the area at midnight, a huge cloud of ash and vapour had spread across the sky. The eruption continued for a month, culminating in a violent explosion which was recorded as far away as Alaska. By then the floor of the caldera had sunk by 1,000 feet and the lake at one end had moved to the other side.

In the seventeenth century the islands were individually named by the British. They were then taken over by Spain, who lost them to Ecuador in 1882. Although Christopher Columbus had never visited them, the Ecuadorians gave the islands new names, all associated with him. To the confusion of visitors, both the English and Ecuadorian names are still used, Isabela being also called Albemarle, for example, and Fernandina being also known as Narborough.

The distances between the various islands, which are scattered over 150 square miles, have particular biological importance. They are just far enough apart to prevent an easy interchange of animal species, yet sufficiently remote from each other to encourage the development of specialization of form and behaviour. We can never be certain how the newly emerged archipelago was colonized by wildlife. Plant seeds and spores were probably wind-borne, or deposited in bird droppings. Plants tolerant of salinity probably floated across from the mainland. Only about one-third of the vegetation of the Galápagos is now endemic, owing to the large number of tropical fruit-bearing and other species which have been artificially introduced by man. These introductions, which are much deplored by scientists, are gradually replacing the native species.

Seabirds were obviously the first animals to colonize the islands, and they probably did so before the emergence of vegetation. Thanks to the upwelling of copious plankton brought from the Antarctic by the cold Humboldt current, the sea around the archipelago is extremely rich in fish. It is not surprising therefore that in addition to various species of boobies, shearwaters, petrels, frigatebirds, gulls and terns, the Galápagos also have their own species of albatross, a penguin and a flightless cormorant, which occur nowhere else in the world. The inexhaustible abundance of food and the absence of predators have enabled the cormorant to dispense with the need for flight.

Terrestrial animals face far greater difficulties in colonizing remote islands. Some could have reached the Galápagos as passengers on the rafts of vegetation and uprooted trees which are carried out to sea from the great rivers of western South America. The fur seals and sealions obviously needed no such assistance; but the ancestors of the giant tortoises may have drifted across by this means. No such enormous creatures inhabit South America, but one of the smaller mainland species was probably their origin. In the absence of competition and predators and by the process of gigantism which is often a feature of island evolution, the original colonists of this species would have been free to develop over the millennia into today's 400-pound monsters.

There are two unique species of iguanas in the Galápagos, one terrestrial and the other marine. The latter, with its crested back and ponderous movements on land, resembles a reincarnated miniature dinosaur. Both are thought to have evolved from the same original mainland terrestrial species. For a land reptile to have accepted a marine existence involved profound physiological changes. Most reptiles live in hot climates. Cold water, and particularly very cold sea water such as the Humboldt current provides around the Galápagos, is anathema to them. They have no such automatic temperature regulating system as is enjoyed by mammals and to survive must therefore contrive to keep within safe limits of both heat and cold. When the marine iguana of the Galápagos is foraging for the algae on which it feeds on the cold seabed, it returns periodically to the sunny rocks on shore to restore its temperature — to recharge its batteries, as it were. Whilst resting, it spits out the salt which it has ingested when feeding under water. Few more extraordinary examples of evolution to enable a totally new environment to be adopted can be found in the animal kingdom.

Colonization by land-birds had to wait for a fairly advanced state of vegetation. We know today that vagrants from the mainland are not infrequently wind-drifted to the Galápagos and this is undoubtedly how the ancestors of the endemic species arrived. One of the earliest successful colonists was a small, insignificant-looking, seed-eating finch. From its off-spring in the course of time have evolved no fewer than thirteen distinct species which, as a group, have become perhaps the most famous little birds in the world — Darwin's finches. Scientists have now divided them into three different genera. It was the appearance and feeding behaviour of these birds which gave Darwin the key to evolution by natural selection.

There is a constant interchange of genes within the population of a mainland species which maintains the stability of its form and behaviour. On remote islands, the genetic pool is restricted and in reproductive isolation the opportunities for the development of new characteristics are far greater. In mainland communities all the available ecological niches are already occupied, but when the pioneers of Darwin's finches reached the islands, they found no competition and the field wide open for specialization. As their numbers increased and with a free choice of ecological niches, they began to spread from island to island, breaking out of the narrow confines which had previously been dictated by inter-specific competition for food and breeding sites. As their evolution progressed, so did the shapes of their bills to enable them to take full advantage of the various new food sources which they found available. Today the bills of Darwin's finches range from the massive, kernel-cracking shape of the large ground-finch *Geospiza magnirostris* to the slender bill of the insect-eating warbler-finch *Certhidea olivacea*, which occupies the niche which would normally be taken by a warbler. One of the finches feeds by probing the calyx of the opuntia cactus flowers with its long bill; another feeds by turning over stones ten to fifteen times its own weight; some of the finches feed on the ground, others in trees, or only in low vegetation. One has taken to the vampire-like habit of taking blood, by pecking the bases of the wing-feathers of the big seabirds. An even more extreme specialization has been developed by the woodpecker-finch, which has learned to use a tool to obtain its favourite food: it breaks off a spine from a cactus and, holding this in its bill, probes for grubs in the beetle-holes in the bark of trees.

A similar course of evolutionary change in physical and

behavioural characteristics can be seen in the giant tortoises, the small iguanid lava lizards, the harmless *Dromicus* snakes and the mockingbirds of the Galápagos, all of which have developed into a number of distinctly different forms on different islands.

Darwin noted the differences in behaviour and bill-shape of the finches (though he apparently did not see them all during his five weeks on the islands) and he pondered them deeply, without at first grasping their full significance. Ten years later he wrote cautiously, 'Seeing the graduation and diversity of structure in one small, intimately related group of birds, one might really fancy that from an original paucity of birds in this archipelago, one species had been taken and modified for different ends.'

He already had the key, but it was not until 1858 that he summoned the courage to turn it. Because of his doubts and religious scruples it is doubtful whether he would have spoken even then had it not been for knowledge that the zoogeographer Wallace had independently reached similar conclusions. So, twenty-two years after writing his field-notes in the Galápagos, the joint announcement of Darwin's and Wallace's views on evolution was made at a meeting of the Linnacan Society in London. Apparently it was quietly received. But a year later, when Darwin's *The Origin of Species* was published, the entire edition was sold on the first day and the effect this time was like the explosion of a bomb. It was this book and his later *The Descent of Man* which caused such violent theological and philosophical controversy. Almost everyone read them with a mixture of fascination, horror and indignation. The revelation that man had not been created intact by God, but was the result of an infinitely long process of gradual change from primitive animal ancestors, was almost impossible for Victorian England to accept. Gilbert and Sullivan were quick to make an appropriate reference in *Princess Ida*:

'Darwinian man, though well behaved,
At best is only a monkey shaved.'

9.

Darwin noted that the wildlife of the Galápagos had no fear of man. A rapid increase in tourism now threatens both the habitat and the behaviour of the wildlife in this remote island paradise.

Top: Galápagos sealions.

Above centre: Mockingbirds.

Below centre: Short-eared owl.

Bottom: Land iguana.

10. A 10-foot Komodo monitor is a powerful carnivore fully capable of killing and eating the deer and pigs which inhabit its island home in Indonesia. *Below*: A male mallee-fowl tests the temperature in its incubator-mound before the female lays an egg. Some mounds are 10 feet high. The eggs are buried and left to hatch 3 feet below the surface.

Darwin was lampooned in the press and denounced from the pulpit. Poor, earnest Darwin — how he and his strictly orthodox wife must have suffered! But a new page had been turned in the progress of science and the arguments he put forward for the common descent of all creatures by what he termed a gradual 'transmutation of species' could not be brushed aside. Such a humbling concept, once accepted, opened the floodgates of knowledge, not only of science, but of man's entire appreciation of the universe. Human history was stripped of its cloying mythology. To quote the rolling conclusion in *The Descent of Man*: 'Man may be excused for feeling some pride at having risen, though not by his own exertions, to the very summit of the organic scale; and the fact of his having thus risen, instead of having been aboriginally placed there, may give him hope for a still higher destiny in the distant future. But we are not concerned here with hopes or fears, only with the truth as far as our vision permits us to discover it.'

The Galápagos Islands are infinitely precious to the civilized world, not only for their association with Darwin's work, but as a laboratory for further studies. Man and his domestic animals have always been the chief threat to their existence. It has been calculated that ship's crews removed at least ten million giant tortoises for food since the islands were discovered. Some of the unique species were thus totally exterminated and several are today very near to extinction. The Galápagos fur seals were only just saved by protective legislation from annihilation by fur traders. Introduced pigs, goats, donkeys, cattle, cats, dogs and rats have become firmly established in a feral state on most of the islands and are devastating the vegetation or killing the indigenous wildlife. Introduced plants are supplanting the native vegetation. In the 1930s the extremely harmful little 'fire ant' *Wasmannia auropunctata* was accidentally introduced from the mainland and is now spreading rapidly from island to island, destroying the endemic insects. Cheap tourism is the latest threat. One of the greatest charms of the Galápagos is the extraordinary tameness of the wildlife (*see* Plate 9). One can pat the sealions or go swimming with them, photograph nesting birds or iguanas at two paces,

9

and have mockingbirds snatch food from one's lips. But when thousands of tourists are doing this, trampling the fragile vegetation and littering the beaches, what will become of the islands then?

The creation of the Charles Darwin Foundation for the Galápagos, with Sir Julian Huxley as its President of Honour, came about in time to curb some of the worst abuses to the islands. Supported by the Ecuadorian Government, UNESCO, the World Wildlife Fund and others, it is gradually reducing the ravages of the feral domestic animals, while at the same time being engaged in an intensive programme of research. With a small resident team of scientists and a research vessel provided by the W.W.F., it has already scored some notable successes, such as breeding the six most gravely endangered tortoises from eggs which would otherwise have been destroyed by pigs. I have been a member of its council for a number of years and am proud of its growing achievements. It is, however, always short of funds and, although it can influence the protection of the wildlife, it has, of course, no executive powers to control the behaviour of the local human inhabitants, whose numbers have now soared to 5,000. Nor should it have, for its work is entirely scientific and educational. The local population and tourism are the responsibilities of the government of Ecuador. The archipelago is now a protected national park, but many serious problems yet remain to be solved.

The Spaniards called the Galápagos 'Las Islas Encantadas' — the enchanted islands. With so many difficulties facing those who are striving to preserve the unique wildlife and the equally unique ethos of the archipelago, how long will this enchantment last? It can survive only if man recognizes, before it is too late, his fatal predilection to destroy with his embrace the very things he most admires.

13 Wallace's Islands

Just as the Galápagos Islands will for ever be identified with Charles Darwin, so must Indonesia be associated with the memory of his contemporary, Alfred Russel Wallace. Here at Ternete in the Moluccas in 1858, while sick with fever, Wallace wrote his famous letter to Darwin, accompanied by the essay on 'The tendency of varieties to depart indefinitely from the original type.' Darwin was bowled over by the shock of learning that Wallace had independently reached the same conclusion as he had about the evolution of species by natural selection. The outcome was, of course, the reading of their joint paper to the Linnaean Society. After the publication of *The Origin of Species* and *The Descent of Man*, the full blaze of world renown enveloped Darwin. Wallace, far from objecting to the relatively little credit given to his own part in the great discovery, treated Darwin as his hero and went out of his way to encourage the limelight to fall on his admired friend.

Nevertheless, Wallace was a phenomenal contributor to science. Whereas Darwin had benefited from a reasonably affluent background and had at least a nodding acquaintance with science before setting out on the *Beagle*, Wallace as a young man lacked both money and scientific training. Beginning life as a surveyor, he supplemented his income by collecting beetles for any museum or private individual willing to pay for his services. Realizing that success would depend on collecting unknown specimens, he set out for the wilds of Brazil, where he spent four arduous years in the remotest jungle he could find. Ill fortune dogged him and on the way home his entire collection was destroyed by fire on board ship. Nothing daunted, he set out again for what in those days was called the Malay Archipelago — today Indonesia. During the following six years, he travelled 14,000 miles by native sailing boat, canoe, or on foot, visiting many hitherto unexplored islands between the Malay Peninsula and New Guinea.

The result of Wallace's work there, some 125,660 specimens of mammals, birds, reptiles, sea-shells and insects, many totally unknown to science, enormously enriched the British Museum of Natural History. His writings, on an amazingly wide range of subjects, and particularly his later contributions on mimicry in nature, evolution and genetics, astonished the scientific world. He has been called the father of zoogeography. One of his observations, that the fauna of the Indonesian islands is of Asian origin only as far east as Bali and Borneo and that it is Australasian eastward of that point, has been proved to be accurate. The zoogeographical division is still known as the Wallace Line.

To my mind, Wallace's *The Malay Archipelago* is one of the most readable scientific classics ever written. Very typically, it is dedicated to Charles Darwin, 'to express my deep admiration for his genius and his works'. Unlike Darwin, whose heavy Victorian prose is humourless and prolix, Wallace wrote with enthusiasm and intellectual excitement about his discoveries. To Darwin, all natives were 'savages'. Wallace's writings show a deep and sensitive interest in the daily lives and problems of the native peoples among whom he worked. Darwin became a hypochondriac in later life. Wallace suffered danger, frequent tropical illnesses and real hardship with extraordinary cheerfulness. He must have been a very likeable man. He was certainly one of the world's most dedicated and remarkable amateur naturalists. I took his book with me when I visited Indonesia. Though more than a hundred years old, it is still incomparably the most enjoyable and informative work on the region yet published.

The 3,677 Indonesian islands are scattered like a broken necklace across 3,000 miles of sea, dividing the Pacific from the Indian Ocean. Some are, of course, both very large and well known, such as Sumatra, Java, Timor, Borneo and Celebes. (I still find it difficult to remember that the last two should now be called Kalimantan and Sulawesi.) Most of the thousands of smaller islands are familiar only to the sailors who ply the uncertain seas among them, or to the natives who crop their coconut palms and turtles.

Many of the islands are of volcanic origin and Indonesia can today claim no fewer than seventy-five active volcanoes. Most of the smaller islands, however, particularly to the east, have been slowly built up from the sea bed by the secretions of billions of tiny polyps — the ever industrious corals, on the crests of whose dead colonies above the life-giving sea, vegetation has gradually established itself. Seen from an aircraft, these sun-drenched atolls are just as beautiful as they are when one sets foot upon them. In the centre is a dark patch of palms and mangroves, encircled by a dazzling white beach of coral sand. Between the beach and the protective outer reef, where the long waves break in thunderous splendour, the lagoon is shallow and from above looks a translucent emerald green. Beyond the reef the coral plunges almost vertically to the ocean bed and there the water is a deep, ultramarine blue.

Landing on an uninhabited island is always a thrilling experience. To discover one where neither the beach nor the island itself reveals a single human footprint or trace of previous occupation, is a joy to be remembered for a lifetime. Some such islands still exist in Indonesian waters.

The lagoons around these islands are usually crystal clear and crowded with an astounding variety of spectacularly colourful tropical fish. During my tour I was accompanied by two experts. One was Nicholas Guppy, a very fine botanist. The other was Rod Salm, a marine biologist from Mozambique, who in one small lagoon identified no fewer than eighty-six different fish species in less than an hour's diving.

Modern ichthyologists have shown both imagination and a sense of humour in selecting names for tropical fish. I was delighted by the list which Rod had written in his underwater notebook as he catalogued his observations. Who can resist such splendid names as the Scribbled Sweetlips, the

Surprised Squirrel-fish, the Stop-and-Stare Fish, the Scissor-
tailed Serjeant-major, or the Thick-lipped Slipperydick? So
much better than the frequent striving for immortality in
bird-names associated with their discoverers, such as White's
Thrush, James's Flamingo, or Radde's Warbler.

On the tiny island of Enu, south of the Aru Islands, we
found surprises of a different kind. As our rubber dinghy
came ashore, I realized that turtle hunters had preceded us.
The beach was littered with the empty carapaces of the animals
they had slaughtered. Following the chevron tracks of the un-
fortunate females to their laboriously excavated nests in the
sand at the edge of the mangroves, we found they had all been
robbed of their eggs. Wherever turtles occur, and their range
is world-wide in the warm seas, they suffer similar persecution.
Not only are they and their eggs taken as a source of food, but
their 'shells' are converted into tourist souvenirs. The survival
of the green, the leathery, the hawksbill and several other
turtle species is now at risk. Even when not persecuted by
man, the reproductive success of turtles is always problematical,
because the watchful frigatebirds and other natural predators
catch the majority of the hatchlings during their perilous three
or four minutes' journey from the nest to the relative safety of
the sea. Yet turtles, as a valuable source of human food, could
be cropped indefinitely if their breeding beaches were not
systematically plundered by man and if controlled quotas for
cropping could be enforced.

Sadly we left the empty beach to explore the island. In the
centre, guarded by dense mangroves, was a brackish pool,
where big, sea-going estuarine crocodiles had left their tracks.
Probably their eggs were hidden somewhere in the muddy
sand among the maze of arching stilt-roots.

Presently, while we were returning to the beach, where the
vegetation was less dense and there were enormous lilies beneath the trees, Nicholas found the first of five unmistakable
nest-mounds of megapodes, averaging five feet high by
twenty wide. All had been robbed of their eggs. I was excited
by the discovery, for megapodes are among the most extraordinary birds in the world.

There are thirteen species of megapodes, ranging from the chicken-size junglefowl (*Megapodius*, not to be confused with the Asiatic junglefowl *Gallus*) to the turkey-size mallee-fowl and brush-turkeys (*Telegallus* and *Aepypodius*). Originating in Australasia, some of them have spread along the off-shore islands as far west as the Nicobar Islands, as far north as the Philippines and as far east as Samoa and Fiji. Their collective name megapode is from the Greek, meaning 'big foot'. All of them have very powerful legs, with which, working backwards, they scrape up a mixture of leaf-litter and sand into huge nest mounds, some even as large as ten feet high by sixty wide.

The nesting of megapodes is unique and one of the wonders of the bird world. The pioneer naturalists in Australasia were at first unwilling to believe their eyes when they came across what they thought to be native burial mounds guarded by strange birds. Wallace, who found megapodes as far west as Borneo and Lombok in his day, described their breeding behaviour quite accurately, though not in detail. The first really thorough study, both in the wild and under laboratory conditions, was made by Harry Frith, one of Australia's most eminent wildlife experts, I am indebted to him for permission to use some of the information given in his remarkable book *The Mallee-fowl*, published in 1962.

Though the behaviour of megapodes differs in detail between species, all of them depend on the heat of the sun, or on a combination of heat provided by fermentation and the sun's heat, to incubate their eggs. At least one species has developed the ultimate eccentricity of using volcanic heat, by nesting inside the craters or on the slopes of active volcanoes.

The mallee-fowl can be taken as a typical example. It begins its eleven-month nesting task in the winter, by digging a pit, or excavating a hollow in an existing nest-mound. This is gradually deepened and widened until it is three or four feet deep and ten feet wide. Leaves and other litter are then scraped from the forest floor into the pit. Finer material including sand is then raked on top and the finished dome is carefully smoothed over. Work is then suspended until the rains come and the mound is well saturated. An egg-chamber is then dug in the top, about two feet deep. This is refilled with a fresh mixture of fine leaf litter and sand. An additional layer of sand two or three feet deep is gradually built on top. The incubator is now ready.

This work has taken several months. The male now tests the temperature of the slowly fermenting egg-chamber every day, by digging and thrusting his head down into it (*see* Plate 10). When the time comes for the female to lay, the male is again involved in heavy work. The abnormally large pinkish eggs are laid at intervals of several days and each time the male has first to excavate a hole two feet deep and, when the egg has been deposited in it, he refills the cavity. Separate holes are made for each of five to a possible maximum of thirty eggs.

According to Harry Frith's observations, the eggs take from fifty to ninety days to hatch. During this long period the birds are daily involved in maintaining around the eggs a temperature of 90° to 96°F. This they do by constant testing, by digging and thrusting their heads into the egg-chamber. If the temperature is too high, they scrape away some of the surface litter; if too low, more is added. The labour involved is great, but even so the rate of hatching success is often no better than 50 per cent.

The final event in this extraordinary sequence is the emergence of the young, which are several feet under the surface when they hatch. Unaided, they have to dig their way out, without the benefit of air to breathe. This takes them anything from two to fifteen hours. Some air may percolate through the surface of the mound, but Frith believes that their condition and breathing remain embryonic until they reach the surface. When they do so, totally exhausted, they tumble down the slope of the mound and totter to the shelter of the nearest vegetation. Within an hour their feathers are dry and they can run. In twenty-four hours, so rapid is the growth of their feathers, that they can fly briefly. Their parents, whose labour in hatching the eggs has been Herculean, have nothing to do with their emergence and if the chicks come across them, they flee in alarm! There is no family bond.

I came across megapode mounds in New Guinea when I was serving there during the last war. During our tour of the Indonesian islands a pair was seen briefly on Manuk Island in the Banda Sea; but to my infinite regret I have never had an opportunity to study their amazing behaviour at the nest.

Another small Indonesian island has a cherished place in my memory — Komodo, the island of dragons. It is the most beautiful of the Nusa Tenggara group, with green and dramatically sculpted volcanic hills. Its single village is inhabited by friendly and curly-haired Muslims, who differ considerably in appearance from the smaller and highly artistic Hindus of Bali.

We anchored off Komodo in the deep Bay of Slawi, which is one of the known breeding grounds of whales, dolphins and giant manta rays. At sunrise the peak of Lehok Boi on the north side of the island looked much higher than its reputed 2,142 feet. At the foot of the forested hills, a shining white beach offered an easy landing. Our objective was a locality known as Wae Nggulung, where a colony of the animals which have made the island famous was said to be easily reached. Here lived the Komodo dragons, or, to give them their proper name, the Komodo monitor lizards *Varanus komodoensis*. There is another, larger colony high on the mountain slope at Poreng and a few occur on two small adjacent islands. Unique in the animal kingdom, these powerful carnivores attain a length of nearly ten feet and are capable of killing and eating the wild pigs and Timor deer which inhabit the island's forest. Their total population is thought to be now fewer than 400 and both they and their island home have been given legal protection.

The walk through the forest was deliciously cool in the early morning and the blossoms on the passion-flower vines were opening to the sun. Junglecocks were still crowing. Spotted doves and barred doves were crooning in the trees and several species of brightly coloured pigeons were feeding eagerly on wild figs. Flocks of sulphur-crested cockatoos raced through the trees, screeching noisily and the rich, fluty voices of orioles were heard in every direction.

Wae Nggulung proved to be nothing more pretentious than a single palm-thatched shelter near a small plantation of maize. Here we were led forward by a native guard, who signalled us to keep silent. Arriving at a small, steep gully, we peered cautiously over the edge, and there below, marching across the sand, was a Komodo dragon — a young one, only four feet in length. It was followed shortly by a larger one, which withdrew again. Soon afterwards a real monster, fully nine feet in length, emerged slowly from the overhanging trees and began feeding on the carcass of a large goat which the guard had tied to a stake. Assuring a sufficient food supply for the monitors was one of his duties.

A fully grown Komodo monitor is an extremely impressive animal. The apparent ease with which the one I was watching ripped the hide from the carcass and bit off huge mouthfuls of flesh, suggested the muscular power of a crocodile (*see* Plate 10). While still lizard-like in form, its heavy, bowed legs and massive head were undeniably prehistoric in appearance. All monitors and lizards have the habit of extending their sensitive, snake-like tongues. This one had a yellow forked tongue as thick as my little finger, which it extended for at least ten inches.

It is greatly to be hoped that the Indonesian Government will recognize the need to improve the protection of Komodo and its dragons. Although on paper a protected reserve, the island was recently visited by an American collector for zoos, who stole five of the dragons, flaunting both the Indonesian law and the American Government's prohibition of the importation of animals protected in their countries of origin.

Our explorations took us later to the eastern Indonesian islands of Aru. The principal village, Dobo, is the centre of the mother-of-pearl trade. Here both the vegetation and the wildlife are obviously much more typical of New Guinea than of western Indonesia. Mammals include several marsupials such as the cuscus, the bandicoot (which looks like a giant shrew but has the fused hind toes of a kangaroo) and the wallaby. Birds include the flightless cassowary and about eighty species typical of New Guinea. There is little doubt that the islands were once part of the Australia–New Guinea continent; the three narrow channels dividing the forested main islands from east to west were evidently once the outlets of mainland rivers, though now separated from New Guinea by 150 miles of very shallow sea.

Both the 'king' and the 'great' birds of paradise were common in the forests in the days of Wallace, who spent six adventurous months there in 1857, but it is doubtful whether many now survive the efforts of the plume hunters and museum collectors. We saw the primitive little wooden house on stilts where Wallace lived and were greeted by the descendants of the Papuans who had been his companions. On a launch trip up one of the rivers we noticed some of them still carrying the bows and blunted arrows which Wallace saw them using to bring down, without damaging their silky plumes, birds of paradise displaying in their courtship trees.

The edges of the forest, which rose like high green walls along the river banks, were full of colourful birds such as the big eclectus parrots, the males of which have startling red and blue plumage and the females emerald green and blue. Sacred kingfishers, which are relatives of the Asiatic white-collared kingfisher, kept passing our launch and we had good views of the enormous black palm cockatoos, which boast the most flamboyant crests of any of this colourful group. Birds feeding on the forest fruits included the Papuan hornbill, the striking black and white Torres Strait pigeons and many noisy channel-billed cuckoos. Violet and green broad-billed rollers, which the Australians call 'dollar-birds', were perched at intervals in the tree-tops. The Aru Islands have a greater variety of interesting birds than any of the Indonesian possessions except perhaps Sumatra and Borneo. The world's most beautiful pigeon — the pale blue crowned pigeon — occurs in these forests. No other bird can compete with its erect, lace-like fan crest. By far the largest and also one of the most self-confident of the pigeons, it allows itself to be easily shot or trapped. I saw four of them, all slightly wounded and tied by the leg, for sale as food in the market at Dobo. Their bright ruby eyes exactly matched the beads of blood which dripped slowly from their wounds. The species is strictly protected in New Guinea, but not in the Aru Islands. It is heartbreaking that for all the fame given to the islands by Wallace more than a century ago, there is still no attempt to protect what remains of their wildlife.

At the time of my visit in 1973, Indonesia was suffering one of the most serious exploitations of wildlife Asia has yet seen. In order to provide for its exploding human population, the government had embarked on a programme of agricultural expansion. Inevitably this involved the destruction of forests. Almost all Indonesian wildlife is directly or indirectly dependent on these forests for food or shelter. Moreover, the magnificent rain forests of western Indonesia, like those of Malaya, grow on soil which is hyper-sensitive to exposure. One teaspoonful of forest soil contains 1,000 million micro-organisms which alone make it capable of transforming indigestible molecular building materials into a form which plants can use. Once the hill forests are clear-felled, the tropical sun oxidizes the organic matter in the soil and the monsoon rains cause severe leaching and erosion, followed by the silting-up of the water drainage and flooding in the valleys (*see* Plate 16).

The temptation to earn quick revenue in the form of hard currency by leasing the Indonesian forests to exploitation by Japanese and Canadian logging companies was perhaps understandable. But the penalties are now coming home to roost. Several of Indonesia's finest wildlife reserves, such as the Kutai in Kalimantan, the homes of the rapidly disappearing orang-utan, the Sumatran rhino, the tiger and other rarities, are now gravely endangered. A current land clearance project in Kutai involves felling a tract of primary forest fifteen kilometres wide into the edge of the reserve. Simultaneously, three major petroleum companies are prospecting for oil in or near the reserve. The invaluable Kinabulu National Park in Sabah (Malayan North Borneo) is similarly threatened by the large-scale extraction of copper ore by a Japanese mining company. Short-term financial gain is assured to Indonesia and Malaya by such ventures. Once completed, however, these countries will not inherit additional land for agriculture, but sterile and eroded land from which the life-giving top-soil and water-retaining forest will have disappeared.

The rain forests of Indonesia and Malaya represent one of the richest natural communities on earth. The scientific and economic importance of this immense but as yet little studied genetic resource, cannot be overestimated. All of the world's fruit trees, spices, commercially exploitable timber trees and plants of medicinal value originated in the wild. All could have had their original stocks destroyed before their value was known, by the blind policy of massive clear-felling which the lumber companies appear to be following in their plunder of south-east Asia.

Perhaps the saddest outcome of my visit to Indonesia was the discovery that the unique Balinese race of the tiger, the smallest of the eight different races of the species, had become extinct and that the Javanese race had been reduced to only five animals. Both were once abundant in their respective islands. Today there are no forest tracts left in Bali large enough to support tigers. In Java the Betiri Forest Reserve, where the last of its tigers remain, must soon feel the pressure of the expanding human population and the growing demand for timber. Meanwhile, last-minute efforts are being made to strengthen its protection.

Bali, with its 10,300-foot volcano Gunung Agung, the 'Navel of the World', is the most precious jewel of the Indonesian possessions. The exotic nature of its rich Malayo-Polynesian culture, the colourful rituals of its innumerable religious ceremonies, the bewitching beauty of its gorgeously attired girl dancers and the constant devotion of its people to artistic pursuits such as carving, weaving, painting, music and dancing, are unique in the world. One could live a lifetime in this small island without seeing all its cultural treasures. Intensely industrious, and deeply religious though firmly believing in dragons and demons, the gentle Balinese make one question some of the values of western civilization. It is a land where even the tiniest village has its temples, every rice-field its little shrine, every gatepost and even every traffic island its beautifully carved beneficent god to ward off misfortune. Life for the Balinese is a perpetual struggle between the forces of good and omnipresent evil. Every decision is subject to religious auspices and every object, even a flower or a stone by the wayside has an individual 'soul', whose influence must be considered. In such a vivid spirit world, one would expect that all wild animals, which most forms of the Hindu religion require to be unmolested, would be flourishing. Unfortunately this is not so. Bali now has two and a half million people crammed into an intensively cultivated island of only seventy miles by thirty and wildlife is vanishing, not by persecution but by lack of habitat. Forests have become paddyfields, watered by the most skilfully devised irrigation system ever constructed by manual labour. It is planned that the number of tourists is to be increased from the present 60,000 a year to 800,000 within the next few years. The surviving wild animals are restricted to the very few remaining patches of forest. Unless the human population explosion subsides or can be brought under control, Bali will have no wildlife except a few monkeys, pigs and rodents. The bird species are now far less numerous than those ornithologists who visited Bali before me have reported.

Indonesia has an impressive list of no fewer than 122 wildlife reserves in its various islands. However, a recent report points out that only thirty-seven of these are larger than two square miles and that even fewer are either fully protected or managed to satisfactory scientific standards. Too much reliance has been placed on the admittedly very fine Udjung Kulon reserve in Java and on the Gunung Leuser in Sumatra, both of which have benefited from substantial financial help from the World Wildlife Fund. Invaluable though these reserves are in protecting the surviving Javan and Sumatran rhinoceroses, the orang-utan and the banteng, they cannot embrace more than a fraction of the long list of disappearing species in Indonesia and neither of them caters for the endangered marine species. In 1972 the government budget for wildlife protection throughout Indonesia, the fifth largest nation in the

world, was equivalent to only about £10,000. It is scarcely surprising therefore that most of the reserves are only partly
effective and that at the time of my visit protective legislation
was being openly flouted. Tigers in Sumatra, though protected by law, were still being shot by visiting Germans and
Americans, undoubtedly with the full knowledge of the local
police. At Dobo, in the Aru Islands, the port authorities made
no effort to prevent the shipment of a whole boat-load of wild-
caught birds and other animals. Birds of paradise, though on
the protected list, were still being exported from Aru and West
Irian. Defenceless dugongs (the 10-foot seal-like mermaids
and sirens of mythology) were being killed in large numbers
in the shallow seas, so that their teeth could be made into
cigarette holders with supposed aphrodisiac benefits to the
smoker.

It is easy to criticize the Indonesians, but there is another
side to the question. Nearly all the exploitation of forests and
mineral resources of the country is being carried out by
Japanese, American, Canadian, Dutch, Swiss, or German
companies. The market for orang-utans and other rare animals
which are being poached in Indonesia is not local, but is almost
exclusively in the western democracies. We have no right to
criticize so long as our own nationals continue to exploit Indonesia's natural treasures for their own gain. Nor can we be
surprised if occasionally an under-paid junior Indonesian
official succumbs to the kind of advertisement recently published by an American collector, who offered $5,000 for one
of the region's rarest reptiles. After all, this represents several
times his annual salary.

A World Wildlife Fund national appeal is in formation in
Indonesia as this book goes to press. The government is
actively co-operating with the International Union for Conservation of Nature and Natural Resources, in devising a new,
ten-year conservation programme. Fifteen additional wildlife
reserves and a marine national park have just been created.
There is already a small number of dedicated and skilled
Indonesian conservationists, who hitherto have had to struggle
against almost insurmountable difficulties. Given this fresh

impetus and with increased assistance from international sources, they may yet stem the terrible losses which have occurred. Very few countries possess such riches as still remain there and every effort should be made to help the Indonesians. But I fear that, because of the widespread destruction of forests, time is running out for the wildlife of Wallace's Islands.

11. As we approached the West Irian coast, the long Asmat war canoes came out to meet us. When we landed, handfuls of lime were thrown in greeting and the whole village turned out to dance around us. The head-hunters of Asmat and New Guinea (*below*) are the last survivors of a unique Stone Age civilization, living in perfect equilibrium with their environment.

12.

Above: Praslin Island in the
Seychelles is the home of the
unique *coco-de-mer* palm,
which bears the largest fruit in
the world.

Left: The lemurs of Grande
Comore are trapped as exhibits
for tourists.

14 The Perfumed Islands

On one of my long-distance flights during the War, I found myself in an infernally noisy and uncomfortable Liberator bomber, in which I was making my way from India by way of Africa, Ascension Island and Brazil to Washington D.C. It would have been far quicker eastward by way of the Philippines, but as this would have involved crossing the Japanese war zone I was condemned to a tiresome journey which, with stops for fuel and changes of crew, would take the best part of four days and nights. I could sleep reasonably well among the mail bags, but spent most of the time in the co-pilot's seat for the sake of company.

For reasons known only to the American pilot, we had swung far south over the Indian Ocean in approaching Africa. I noticed on the horizon to the left a small group of islands. I pointed, with a questioning look at the pilot. 'The Comoros,' he shouted, just audible above the roar of the engines. The tiny islands looked green and inviting, with their white beaches and long lines of breaking surf.

Twenty-five years later, in the comfort of the s.s. *Lindblad Explorer*, I paid my first visit to these enchanting spice islands. We had just spent an adventurous two days exploring Aldabra, a rather hostile little atoll protected by treacherous reefs and flotillas of enormous sharks. On the first day a violent storm had all but capsized our rubber landing craft. Aldabra and its 100,000 giant tortoises and many rare birds is now a closely guarded and invaluable centre of island wildlife research.

The Comoros are of volcanic origin. We had seen the 8,000-foot peak of their highest mountain, Mount Karthala, on the horizon long before the islands themselves came into view. There are four main islands and a number of small ones. Grande Comore, with its capital Moroni, is the largest — about 450 square miles. Next come the much smaller Anjouan and Mayotte and finally Mohéli, only eighty square miles. The French, who took possession in 1841, call them '*Les Comores — L'Archipel des Parfums*', which is an admirable description bearing in mind that 70 per cent of their exports are highly aromatic spices and fruits. These include cloves, nutmegs, vanilla, cinnamon, lyang-lyang, tuberose, patchouli, lemon grass and oranges. All of these were introduced into the Comoros many centuries ago by the seafaring Arabian traders, who in turn obtained them from the spice islands of the Dutch East Indies.

The inhabitants of the Comoros are of mixed descent from the early Arabian settlers, Malagasys, Negro slaves and European adventurers. In the old days the islanders had a great reputation as pirates and ship-wreckers among the traders who sailed the Mozambique Channel. The 'Black Pirates' of the Comoros were in fact the terror of the western Indian Ocean. Today the people are mostly charming and happy-go-lucky. Their religion is basically Comoroan-Islamic; but witchcraft not unlike that of Haiti is still practised in the country areas.

The wildlife of the islands is of considerable interest, though confused by large numbers of artificial introductions from Malagasy, Africa and India. The birds, such as can escape the guns, slings, catapults and traps of the islanders, include a number of endemic species, as well as forms which probably originated in the Mascarene Islands or Malagasy. C. W. Benson, who led the Centenary Expedition of the British Ornithologists' Union to the Comoros in 1958, recorded only seventy bird species, but was there at a time when marine birds were scarce. A. D. Forbes-Watson, who was collecting for the Smithsonian Institution in 1969, identified eighty-four. Separate visits by the American naturalist Doctor Roger Tory Peterson and myself in 1971 both resulted in lists of eighty-two, including a few obvious vagrants. As none of us visited all the smaller islands, nor had sufficient time for a complete survey, the real total may be around ninety or more. Considering the fairly modest size of the islands and the extent to which the vegetation has been degraded by long human occupation, such a total compares very favourably with those of other archipelagos in the Indian Ocean.

Among the rather few mammals of the islands, a wild lemur on Grande Comore is of particular interest (*see* Plate 12). As the home of sixteen of the lemur species is in Malagasy, some 300 miles away, I suspect that the one in the forests of Grande Comore is descended from animals released by the earlier settlers. Unfortunately it is often trapped as a tourist attraction.

Though colourful, Grande Comore is in parts very arid and heavily scarred by lava flows. One small volcano is still active. The harbours, with their Arab dhows, pirogues and outrigger canoes are irresistible to any photographer. The older parts of Moroni, with its narrow, twisting alleys, dazzling white flat-roofed houses and picturesque mosques, is also very photogenic, though to me less interesting than the uninhabited regions.

One of the most enjoyable excursions I made was along the coast road to the so-called Salt Lake, which is a deep and high-rimmed crater lake heavily impregnated with sulphur. Viewed from the edge of its rim, the water looks a dark indigo colour, contrasting sharply with the brilliant cobalt blue of the nearby sea. The almost vertical sides of the caldera are inhabited by about a thousand large fruit bats, which fly with slow, crow-like wing-beats over the lake, their bright chestnut bodies gleaming in the sun. Along the road to the lake through the lava flows of the 1918 eruption of an adjacent volcano, stand a number of ancient baobab trees, with gigantic, swollen trunks as large as any I have seen in Africa. Some are ten or twelve feet thick and with their few small, root-like branches sprouting apologetically at the summit, well live up to their popular name of 'upside-down trees'. Their pale grey adipose trunks store a lot of water and during droughts in Africa the elephants gouge huge holes in them with their tusks in order to chew the juicy pulp, eventually destroying the trees.

Of the four main islands, by far the most beautiful and verdant is Anjouan, known as 'The Pearl of the Comoros'. Because of its extremely fertile soil and high rainfall it is also the most densely populated, with 100,000 inhabitants. Some areas of the original luxuriant forest have survived in the highlands and it was here that I saw the interesting vasa parrots and the big blue Comoro pigeons. The highest peak, Mount N'tingui, dominates the view and there are some very beautiful high waterfalls at Tatinga. In the harbour town of Mutsamudu are fine examples of seventeenth-century buildings and curiously cone-shaped tombs. In the markets the exotic display of fruits, vegetables and spices and the colourful costumes of the women are an attractive spectacle. The typical costume of the women of Anjouan is a wide, all-enveloping garment, usually boldly patterned in red and white, which covers them from head to toe. Like all Muslims, the women are very modest and cover their faces in the presence of strangers. As they approach, they raise the upper folds of their robes, holding them at eye level with arms extended sideways, leaving just a half-inch slit beneath the hood through which their dark eyes peep. This gives them a square, box-like shape as they sail past, like galleons under full canvas. It is a quaint and engaging custom which I have seen in no other Muslim country.

Anjouan affords an opportunity to see most of the world's spices growing in plantations. How much more beautiful and interesting they are as plants than as the horrid little dried vestiges which are used in the kitchens of our homes! There is a kind of Arabian-nights effect in seeing long lines of graceful women carrying on their heads baskets full of nutmegs, cinnamon, jasmine flowers or cloves on their way to market. When the lyang-lyang bushes are being stripped of their greenish-yellow blossoms, the sweet scent fills the air for half a mile around.

The off-shore waters of Anjouan are, of course, the home of the famous coelocanth. The first of these prehistoric-relic fish was caught off the South African coast, evidently as a vagrant as no fewer than six were since then caught off Anjouan, which suggests that this is their main breeding area. It is strange that this unique creature with limb-like fins was discovered alive only so recently by scientists, who previously knew of its existence only from fossils dating back some 300 million years. However, the native fishermen of Anjouan have apparently known the living fish long enough to have given it a name — the *gombessa djomole*.

Like Anjouan, the neighbouring island of Mohéli contains rich pastures and some original forest. Though the smallest of the main islands, it was the one most favoured by the early navigators because of the sheltered anchorage provided by the screen of adjacent Mioumachoua islets. The coast is extremely beautiful, with deeply curved bays and superb sand beaches overhung by graceful coconut palms. Here I found many interesting birds such as the Madagascar green pigeon, the malachite kingfisher and the indigenous Comoro thrush.

Mayotte, the fourth large island, is a typical volcanic plug and in geological terms is probably the oldest of the group. It also had the worst reputation among seafarers, both because of its treacherous reefs and the notorious skill of the local Mahorais as wreckers and looters. It was nevertheless a favourite target of the slave traders of Malagasy and Zanzibar, who decimated the island's population. Its contours are rugged and show evidence of heavy erosion. There is a substantial crater lake named Dziani on the neighbouring islet of Pamanzi. Another islet, Dzaoudzi, is guarded by an interesting battery of ancient wheeled cannons; its village square swarms with grey-headed lovebirds, an introduced species which is now feral and obviously thriving. Apart from considerable numbers of yellow-bellied sunbirds, the most beautiful bird I saw here was a Madagascan paradise flycatcher, whose grotesquely long tail had attracted the attention of small boys armed with slings; fortunately they failed to hit so small a target.

The great lagoon of transparent water behind the reef at Mayotte is a paradise for the under-water photographer. It is as crowded with brilliantly coloured tropical fish, sea anemones and corals as any in the Indian Ocean. The beaches are similarly treasure stores of colourful and wonderfully shaped shells of countless kinds. Unhappily the Comoro islanders, like those of the Seychelles, have learned that such things can be sold very profitably to tourists and the collecting of living marine creatures in order to obtain their shells is already a worrying factor. Spear fishing is actively promoted by the tourist board and it will not be long before the lagoons and reefs are as denuded as those of many Caribbean islands. Beyond the reefs of the Comoros, tourists are able to enjoy fishing for enormous sail-fish, barracuda, caranx and other deep-water game fish.

I hope that the government of the Comoros will one day learn from the examples of the Seychelles and Mozambique that the creation of marine national parks is a wise as well as a profitable venture. From an economic viewpoint alone the national treasures of the in-shore waters are worth far more as perpetual attractions to tourists who wish to see them, than can be gained in the few years before the tourists who now kill or collect them have destroyed the resource. Most tourists are perfectly happy to respect conservation laws, providing that they are given opportunity to see and photograph wildlife in reserves. Marine reserves are no exception and the conversion from harpoon guns to the now easily acquired and easily operated under-water cameras is not difficult to bring about. Indeed the sale of such equipment to tourists visiting marine reserves can be a profitable source of income for paying the wages of the necessary guards.

The Comoros, like the Seychelles, are fortunately still fairly rich in natural treasures of many kinds, in spite of intensive cultivation and rapidly increasing human populations. It is not too late to save what remains. The government of the Seychelles has recognized this by introducing a fine programme of conservation which embraces both terrestrial and marine resources. What awaits the Comoros if its government does not take conservation more seriously can be seen on another archipelago, the Mascarenes, which lie to the east of Malagasy.

The Mascarene archipelago was once famous as the home of the now long extinct dodo and the solitaires. Today it provides a terrible object lesson to conservationists. One of the three main islands, Rodrigues, has lost virtually all of its original vegetation and is now over-populated, over-grazed and heavily eroded. Goats and rabbits effectively prevent any natural regeneration. Only two of its endemic bird species survive. Mauritius and Réunion, which were once rich in forests and unique wildlife species, still have some native forests in areas too difficult to cultivate, but for the most part have been converted to plantations. The economy of Mauritius is 90 per cent dependent on sugar-cane. Both islands have lost most of their endemic fauna. Seven of the few surviving bird species of Mauritius, and five of those on Réunion, are now listed as nearing extinction. There are only five of the beautiful Mauritius kestrels left and only thirty of its pink pigeons. The losses have all been caused, like those of the dodo and solitaires, by man and his introduced predatory animals, or by the conversion of natural vegetation to monocultures of sugar-cane, tea, or other commercial crops.

Little can now be done to restore Rodrigues, but on Mauritius and Réunion last-minute efforts are being made to introduce conservation measures. In the case of Mauritius, the British Government is interested in supporting a local initiative to create a national park to protect the forested Black River gorges. On Réunion there is a growing interest in conservation and some biological reserves have been created, in spite of the growing demands for more land for cultivation. But the proposal of the French Government to introduce exotic game to attract hunting tourists, instead of concentrating on the restoration of the surviving native fauna and flora will, if implemented, be a disastrous error. There is ample evidence from New Zealand, Hawaii and a host of other countries which have indulged in exotic introductions, that they almost invariably result in damage to the biotic community and in surplanting native species.

Both Mauritius and Réunion have embarked on major tourist developments to sustain their economies, but so little now survives of the original beauty and interest of the islands that tourists are going to have some difficulty in distinguishing them from any other largely man-made resorts of the Indian Ocean. Perhaps, so long as the sun shines, the sea-bathing is good and the hotels provide the standardized amenities which tourists demand, they will not mind and the Mascarenes will get their fair share of the tourist bonanza anyway. But to the scientific world and those interested in conservation, the losses which have occurred in these islands and which seem likely to continue to occur, are matters of deep concern.

On a later tour of the islands of the Indian Ocean I had an opportunity to visit Zanzibar, an island whose name alone holds a certain magic. In spite of all the sinister aspects of its past as a centre of despotism and slave trading, it is nevertheless both a beautiful and a romantic place. It is the largest of the in-shore coralline islands of the East African coast, some fifty-three miles long and twenty-four broad. Tanzania is only twenty-two miles distant. In such a strategic location, Zanzibar dominated the coastal sea traffic in the days of sail. Its sultans wielded considerable power and there was an old Arab saying that when anyone in Zanzibar played the flute all Africa as far as the Great Lakes danced. The island was under the influence of the rulers of the Persian Gulf countries long before the birth of Christ. In 1503 it was taken by Portugal, who held it until 1698, when the rulers of Oman regained control. From 1861 until the East African countries achieved independence, it was under British influence, having become a protectorate in 1890. Slave trading, which had provided much of its wealth, was officially abolished in 1897, though continuing clandestinely long afterwards. The Victorian British replaced the infamous slave market by a coral-built Anglican cathedral, though part of the market remains as a tourist attraction. The island's fortunes are now closely linked with those of Tanzania and there is considerable Chinese influence over its development under a foreign aid programme.

Zanzibar's people are of Arab, Indian and African stock. Most of the declining numbers of descendants of the original Bantu-speaking early settlers are now squeezed into the remoter coastal areas, where they are chiefly engaged in fishing or cattle raising. At the time of my visit, commerce was still largely in the hands of the industrious Indians, though the effects of Uganda's and Tanzania's ugly Africanization campaigns were already being felt. The bazaars were full of beautifully worked early Arab silver and Indian carvings and, of course, of the fascinating brass-studded and intricately carved chests for which Zanzibar is famous. Nowhere else in the world can one see such magnificently carved and studded doors as in the old parts of the capital. I was relieved to see that this highly skilled craft has not been lost, but is still being richly applied to the doors and lintels of the new, modern-style banks and civic buildings.

Beyond the fast changing capital city, the island still retains some of the picturesque scenery described by Livingstone, whose white house in Malawi Road still stands. The eccentric Richard Burton also left vivid descriptions of Zanzibar, written when he was recruiting his band of slaves and brigands who accompanied him on his expedition to seek the source of the Nile in 1857. The very fine local museum contains a great number of relics and documents of the age of exploration and of the early period of the sultans, as well as an interesting natural history collection. The old Maruhubi Palace of the sultans is now in ruins, surrounded by ancient kapok and flamboyant trees. It is scheduled for development as a State-owned tourist restaurant, which seems a sad ending to its former magnificence.

I unfortunately did not have time for more than a cursory inspection of the wildlife of Zanzibar. There are a few vestiges of the original tropical forest left, but both the eastern and western parts of the island have been reduced to low scrub or cultivation. About 80 per cent of the world's cloves are raised in Zanzibar and copra is, in tonnage, the main export. The birds are, of course, almost entirely typical East African species, though many long-range migrants also occur, particularly among shore birds. The mammals are more interesting. There used to be a small population of the colobus monkey *Colobus kirkii*, which was said to be distinct from the African mainland species, but I fear it has been exterminated by the skin traders. A similar fate has befallen the suni, a miniature antelope which once inhabited the coastal regions and two of the off-shore islands. The eighteen-inch elephant shrew was first described from a Zanzibar specimen and still survives there. A few leopards remain in the forests, where bush-pigs seemed plentiful. I saw captive specimens of the two native lemur species, which I thought probably conspecific with those of Malagasy. Squirrels, mongooses and civets appeared to be fairly numerous, but I failed to see the genet which is said to inhabit the island. Neither could I find any of the local giant rats, though small rodents were common in the plantations. Skins of locally killed rock pythons and monitor lizards were on sale in the bazaars and I was told that several species of poisonous snakes, including cobras, were occasionally found.

I could discover no evidence of local interest of any kind in conservation. Though certainly a romantic and in parts still beautiful island, Zanzibar gave me the impression of being vigorously exploited without apparent regard for the long-term survival of either forests or wildlife. It is strange that the object lesson of Tanzania's world famous and economically important national parks, such as the Serengeti, the Ngorongoro and the Lake Manyara, has apparently had no influence on those who plan Zanzibar's future. Like some of the other spice islands, Zanzibar may soon find it has no natural treasures left to save.

15 *Man as a Predator*

The early hominids, down to Dr Louis Leakey's so-called 'Nutcracker Man' were undoubtedly vegetarians. On the other hand most of our later Australopithecine forebears were at least partly carnivorous. Modern man is omnivorous, with a carnivorous preference. So long as he remained a rare and highly vulnerable species, fighting for survival among the host of powerful predatory animals which then dominated the world, he was glad to eat anything he could subdue in the way of mammals, birds, reptiles, or fishes, as well as eating vegetables, insects and crustaceans. Though most of us no longer find reptiles or insects acceptable, there are many people in four continents who still eat them with relish. I certainly felt none the worse for sampling dried locusts in Jordan, or from eating a steak of unidentified snake in Burma.

The earliest cave paintings of the Cro-magnons at Le Moustier and Lascaux provide abundant evidence that the joy of hunting had already been firmly established in the Palaeolithic Age. When, some thousands of years later, Neolithic man learned to domesticate some of the herbivorous animals which he hunted and created the first settled communities, the picture began to change. Instead of merely defending himself and his family from the dominant predators such as tigers, lions and bears, he now had also to defend his domestic stock. Moreover, by creating artificial herds in enclosures, he actually stimulated the attacks of hungry predators. The big carnivores, instead of being merely his natural enemies, were also his competitors for the animals which he hunted, either for food or as a social activity. As his weapons and hunting skills improved, he began gradually to reverse the roles. Man and his tribes emerged as the leading predators and soon no wild animal, no matter how large or ferocious, was able to withstand his attack.

The present century has seen the culmination of a long process which began in the Stone Age. From learning to dominate his natural predators, stemmed man's gradual control of his natural environment and ultimately his dominion over the entire biosphere. Although he is still obliged in some parts of the world to kill carnivores and other animals in self defence, this has become the rare exception. The killing in which he still indulges is now almost entirely either for pleasure or for economic gain. He has become the super-predator and the wilful destroyer, not merely of animals potentially harmful of his interests, or useful as providers of food or skins, but of creatures great or small, harmful or inoffensive, which enable him to indulge his deep-rooted hunting instincts.

Just how large a factor killing for pleasure has become is illustrated by the fact that in a single country, the United States, where hunting is now closely restricted, nine to twelve million ducks and geese are shot each year. Of these, four million are mallards. And in every country where this one species occurs, from North America across Europe and Asia, it is again a favourite target. The killing of small birds is also on a gigantic scale. Italy and Cyprus alone accounting for the deaths of several million song-birds every year. Millions of small birds are caught each year for the cage-bird trade. In Bangkok alone the annual catch is put at 300,000, while until very recently, Belgium and France netted several millions.

The role of the predator in nature is important and useful. The large carnivores at the top of the 'food chain', such as the big cats, the eagles and the large owls, though rarely directly controlling the numbers in the populations of their prey species, contribute to the health of their breeding stocks by culling the sick, aged, or weakly individuals, which are the most easily caught.

Natural predation has a built-in self-regulating factor which prevents any one species from multiplying to such an extent as to endanger the community. If a carnivorous predator succeeds in killing all the prey species within its area, its own population immediately declines. Similarly, if grazing animals in a wild state become so numerous as to destroy their habitat, shortage of food brings down their numbers so that the habitat recovers. Man, who is far more mobile, is inhibited by no such controls over his predation on wildlife. Long before the white man and his accurate long-range weapons reached Africa or Asia, the native hunters had already destroyed the natural balance of animal communities, not merely by hunting, but by the use of fire to clear forests and savanna for their grazing animals. The North American Indians changed the whole face of what are now known as the Great Plains, by the extensive burning of forests to extend the feeding area of the bison, on which they depended for meat and hides.

The late James Fisher, for whose scholarly studies of the histories of animals I have unbounded admiration, produced an analysis of the extinction of species, which showed that only one quarter of the 130 species of mammals and birds which have disappeared since AD 1600 (when reliable records began to be made) did so by natural causes. Directly or indirectly, man was responsible for the extinction of the remainder. Natural extinction is part of the evolutionary process. Species can die out by over-specialization, as occurred with the dinosaurs, or by failure to adapt themselves to climatic or other changes such as the pressure of competition from more successful species. Extinction by man can be traced to three main causes: hunting, the artificial introduction of new predators or of domestic animals which compete with the local fauna for food or living space, and the destruction of natural habitats. Fisher's analysis showed that hunting accounted for 33 per cent of all the mammal species which had become extinct since 1600 and for 42 per cent of the birds. Today it is the destruction of habitats which has become the main factor.

The *Red Book of Endangered Species*, published by the International Union for Conservation of Nature, now lists 343 species or distinctive subspecies of mammals and 474 birds as in danger of extinction. The rate at which species are disappearing is therefore obviously and rapidly increasing. The great majority of those now endangered have been brought to this condition by man's influence.

Two classic examples of 'over-kill' which have been amply documented by Professor Jean Dorst and others, occurred in North America. In the other continents wildlife was able to some extent to adapt itself to the steadily increasing pressure of man; but the colonization of North America by the white man was so sudden and on such a rapidly increasing scale that its impact was devastating. The bison, or buffalo, was the first to suffer. In the early part of the nineteenth century there were at least 70 million bison between Lake Erie across the Great Plains to Texas. By 1889 only 541 remained. The slaughter was on an unprecedented scale and was highly organized. At first it was concerned only with the acquisition of land for farming by the early pioneers and with commercial gain from the sale of meat, hides and bones. From 1830 onwards, however, official policy dictated the extermination of the bison in order to starve the native Indians of food and hides and thus subjugate them and obtain their tribal lands. Towards the end, trainloads of city men were offered the 'sport' of shooting unlimited numbers of bison without the inconvenience of leaving the prairie trains. Sometimes the tongues of the bison were taken as delicacies, but more often during this period tens of thousands of carcasses were simply left where they fell. Since those barbarous days, strenuous efforts have been made to save the bison from extinction, by the creation of several well-managed reserves for them. In spite of initial further losses from disease, the species is now multiplying again in a very encouraging manner.

The example of the American passenger pigeon had no such happy ending. This gregarious, long-tailed bird bred in enormous numbers in southern Canada and the eastern United States. Its colonies were so large that trees sometimes collapsed under their weight. A single flock was calculated in 1810 at 2,230 million birds. No other species in North America could compete with its numbers, on which neither the Indians nor the early settlers had made any effect. Commercial enterprise then took a hand and thousands of barrels of pigeons began to be sold for food in the growing cities. Trees were felled in order to obtain the fat nestlings from the countless nests. Farmers whose crops were damaged by the birds joined in the massive slaughter and dynamited the crowded roosting places. By 1870 passenger pigeons had been restricted to the Great Lakes area and by 1899 the species was extinct in the wild. The last zoo specimen died in 1914. Another species, the green and orange Carolina parakeet, which was common throughout the south-eastern United States, was also exterminated completely by man during this brief period.

The money to be made by exploiting wildlife has always attracted American enterprise. The beautiful egrets were very nearly exterminated by plume hunters when the wearing of 'aigrettes' was fashionable. Recently there was a much publicized prosecution of one of America's largest importers of furs. The company concerned was said to have been responsible for about half of the skins smuggled into the United States from Brazil, Mexico and Africa in contravention of the Lacey Act, which forbids the entry of skins of all animals protected by law in their countries of origin. In the space of eighteen months the company had imported as 'hides', through Canadian and Swiss intermediaries, the skins of 46,181 margays, 30,068 ocelots, 15,470 otters, 5,644 leopards, 1,939 jaguars, 1,867 cheetahs, 468 pumas and 217 giant otters. All these species are classified as endangered. But for the vigilance of a PanAmerican airline official, who discovered that a bale of 'hides' was composed of leopard skins, this massive and carefully organized smuggling would doubtless still be continuing.

It is not, of course, only from North America that such examples can be drawn. They have occurred in every continent. In Europe the magnificent aurochs cattle were exterminated by 1627 and the European bison, which had been reduced to just three animals by 1927, was saved from extinction only by intensive captive breeding in zoos. A long list of other species of European mammals and birds which used to be common have disappeared from most of the countries they once occupied and are now surviving in very small numbers in single or very few localities. Europe shares with North America the responsibility for exterminating the last of the great auks, which once flourished in colonies on both shores of the North Atlantic. Boatloads of these defenceless, flightless birds were still being taken until the early part of the eighteenth century, the last survivor being killed in Iceland in 1844. But fewer species have become extinct in Europe than elsewhere, because the expansion of the human population has taken place more slowly and over a longer period than, for example, in North America or Australia.

Africa suffered, on a smaller scale, from a similar sudden incursion of the white man and his weapons as had caused such havoc among North American wildlife. Many species had already been driven out of North Africa by the late eighteenth century and much of the continent had suffered from shifting cultivation, bush fires and over-grazing before the white man began to take his toll. It was in South Africa in the latter part of the eighteenth century where the blow fell heaviest. By the beginning of the nineteenth century the elegant bluebuck was extinct. By 1870 the last of the zebra-like quaggas was shot and shortly afterwards Burchell's zebra met the same fate. The policy of the Boers was to massacre every animal which interfered with their development of farmlands and nothing was spared. The springbok, the blesbok and the bontebok, which had roamed the plains in vast numbers, were almost wiped out; the elephant, the white-tailed gnu and the mountain zebra were also driven out or exterminated. Elsewhere in Africa a similar slaughter began. Elephants and rhinoceroses were shot in thousands as the demand for ivory and rhino horn increased. The trade in hides, furs, meat and mounted trophies rapidly attracted more and more white hunters, who vied with each other in obtaining record bags. Rich men from every part of the world hastened to Africa to share the apparently unlimited opportunities for slaughtering lions, giraffes, buffaloes and countless other species of animals which still offered targets. The tide did not turn until the evidence of over-kill could no longer be denied. Such legalized hunting as is now continuing

13. Bird Island, in the Seychelles, where a million sooty terns nest, used to be heavily exploited by natives who collected the eggs. Today they are protected. *Below*: The delightful little fairy terns in the Cousin Island Reserve lay their single eggs precariously balanced on the branches or trunks of trees, where many are eaten by geckos or are dislodged.

14. The last of the Asiatic lions are now safe in the Gir Reserve in India. In recent years the population has been increased by skilled management from 177 to 217. *Below*: One of the world's most beautiful birds, the blue crowned pigeon, is strictly protected in New Guinea, but in Indonesia's adjacent Aru Islands it is still sold as food.

in Africa is on the whole well controlled by most of the local governments, though poaching remains an intractable problem. Large numbers of well-managed reserves are helping to prevent the further extinction of species.

By comparison with Africa, Asia presents a slightly less discouraging picture, though here, too, wildlife has declined because of the destruction of forests and excessive hunting. The Indian subcontinent, the Malay peninsula and the adjoining Indonesian islands have been the only regions to suffer serious losses from uncontrolled hunting by white men, though in recent times this pressure has been chiefly at the hands of the local nationals. Many Asiatic countries have religious scruples which protect animal life to a considerable extent and there has until recently been less deliberate killing of wildlife in order to make way for agriculture. The exceptions were in China and Asiatic Russia, where extensive land reclamation was accompanied by planned efforts to exterminate many animals, including the Chinese, Siberian and Caspian races of the tiger, though the remnant populations are now protected.

Recurrent warfare has taken a heavy toll of all the larger animals in many Asiatic countries, particularly in the Indo-Chinese region. It has also increased to a dangerous level the already large numbers of accurate firearms in the hands of primitive people, the effect of which is now being felt by the fur-bearing animals, the rhinoceroses and the larger deer species. Already the snow leopard, golden cat, tiger, many of the Himalayan wild sheep and goats and eleven deer are in the *Red Book of Endangered Species*.

Among the many species in danger of extinction is the Asiatic Lion (*see* Plate 14). In 1969, when I visited the Gir Reserve in Gujarat State, where the last of these animals have sanctuary, their total population had dropped to only 177. The reserve was in a critical state. Local villagers had been permitted to extend their grazing and cultivation right across the reserve. Most of the wild deer had disappeared and the lions were obliged to feed on domestic cattle. When they did so, the carcasses were quickly seized by the local *harijans* (low caste people), for the sake of the meat, hides and bones. The lions therefore seldom got a square meal. Recommendations which Dr Paul Joslin and I made to the Gujarat State Government and to Mrs Ghandi, resulted in radical changes in the management of the reserve and the population of lions has since been increased to 217. Thanks to the quick action of the Gujarat officials, the Asiatic lion now looks relatively safe. But the Asiatic cheetah, which was once abundant, has been exterminated everywhere in Asia except for a small number in Iran and possibly also in the Mekran coastal area of Baluchistan. In the African continent, though now protected, it is becoming increasingly rare. There are many other Asiatic species near the brink of extinction, such as Przewalski's Mongolian wild horse, the Bactrian camel, the wild ass, or onager, and the Arabian oryx.*

Recognition of the need to save wildlife came late to Australasia. Its native birds and mammals, and particularly its large number of unique marsupials, had suffered heavy losses long before anything was done to save them. No fewer than thirty-five marsupial species are now on the danger list and several are probably extinct. Some, such as the endearingly toy-like koalas, the bandicoots and a number of species of kangaroos were ruthlessly hunted for their fur. In the 1920s koala skins were still being exported at a rate of hundreds of thousands a year. Today only a few thousand carefully protected koalas remain. The larger kangaroos were the subject of commercially sponsored hunting on a quite extraordinary scale, to provide meat for the cat and dog canned food industry. The only large carnivore of Australasia, the thylacine, or Tasmanian 'tiger', was fiercely persecuted as soon as sheep were introduced into Tasmania. With a bounty on its head, it was exterminated by 1933. This was a unique, dog-like marsupial with a stiff tail and very powerful jaws. Though undoubtedly a sheep-killer, its loss to science was a major tragedy. The dingos, or feral domestic dogs, are now being almost equally persecuted. The many interesting marsupials might have benefited by this

---

* *The rescue and successful breeding of the Arabian Oryx in captivity is one of the great successes of the World Wildlife Fund.*

reduction in their natural predators had it not been for the introduction of foxes, dogs and cats by the settlers with the object of keeping down the rabbits, which they had also introduced. These foreign predators quickly became feral and caused terrible losses among the completely defenceless marsupials, while the invading rabbits destroyed the grazing on which the herbivorous marsupials depended.

The birds of Australasia also suffered severe predation by man and many have become extinct. The *Red Book* lists forty-one species as endangered today. The flightless emus, which used to be mown down with machine-guns during the 'emu war' of 1932, still survive in some parts of Australia and there are still cassowaries in New Guinea, but the unique black emu of King Island and the Tasmanian emu disappeared in the nineteenth century. Many of the brilliantly coloured parrots, cockatoos and parakeets have suffered greatly at the hands of commercial collectors. Even today small species are sold to wealthy collectors for as much as £250 a pair. The golden-shouldered parrot of Cape York, a very rare and strictly protected species, is under constant pressure, a captured pair having recently changed hands for nearly £2,000. Birds of paradise, though now protected throughout their entire range, are still being smuggled out through West Irian to the Asian markets. Since the first Polynesian colonists reached New Zealand, forty-three species of its native birds have disappeared and about a dozen more are now nearing extinction. Only the Hawaiian islands have a worse record, 80 per cent of their endemic land birds now being extinct.

Throughout Australasia, conservationists are now hard at work trying to repair the ravages of the past. Legislation is continually improving to protect wildlife and many fine new reserves have been created. To repay these efforts, several exciting re-discoveries have been made of species thought to be extinct, notably the beautiful little Leadbeater's opossum, the colourful takahe (a flightless gallinule) of New Zealand, and the noisy scrub-bird of western Australia, in whose protection the Duke of Edinburgh played an important role during one of his visits. The last mentioned insignificant little bird is the only one in history to have been saved by siting a proposed new town in a different location in order to protect its habitat!

South America did not suffer the fate of the other continents until more recent times, though all its native humans have always been hunters. Whereas the natives killed only for food, or adornment, the white man hunted for pleasure or financial gain. It was he who developed the multi-million-dollar trade in the skins of jaguars, ocelots, margays, chinchillas, giant otters and vicuñas, all of which are now heading for extinction. He also developed the almost equally lucrative trade in South American monkeys, birds, reptiles, butterflies, and orchids, which until very recently earned fortunes for exporters and importers alike. I gained a first-hand impression of the dimensions of this nefarious industry in 1969 when I visited a German exporter in Bogotá. That morning he was sending to Florida two plane-loads of wild-caught birds from Colombia, Ecuador and Brazil. He informed me proudly that there were 26,000 birds in the grossly overcrowded cages, many of which were already dead or dying as the crates were being loaded. He remarked that normally about 25 per cent died within a week and that the remainder would probably die within a few months, because the great majority of purchasers would not know how to look after them properly. 'But,' he shrugged, 'that's their problem. I am paid in good American dollars!' Among the shipment I noticed rarities such as the quetzal and cock-of-the-rock, both of which birds are strictly protected, as well as several thousand hummingbirds. As I left the premises, thirteen native catchers were carrying in more cages of birds, monkeys and other small animals. The exporter paid them well and equipped them with mist-nets and traps. The depredations of this one small company represent, of course, only a tiny fraction of a world-wide trade which is currently shipping 300 million wild-caught animals each year to pet shops, zoos and medical research centres.

South America is now one of the most heavily exploited continents. Timber extraction, followed by hordes of ravenous goats, is causing not only major losses of wildlife but serious soil erosion. The valuable sandalwood tree is already extinct in the wild and many other species of trees and plants are endangered. The construction of the new Pan-American high-way through Brazil's once impenetrable Mato Grosso is bringing with it the familiar tragedy of progressive exploitation by settlers. As industrialization advances, we must expect even greater conservation problems to arise. Most of the South American countries now have important wildlife reserves, but the effort is tragically late.

The oceans of the world have suffered no less than the land from the predatory behaviour of man. The near extermination of several whale species, which in spite of every international effort is still continuing because of the greed of Japan and the Soviet Union, is now too well known to need description. Persistent overfishing is endangering the future of large numbers of fish species, such as the cod, halibut, herring, sardine and salmon, all of which are important sources of human food. Even the Arctic and Antarctic have not escaped. Although the frightful slaughter of seals, sealions, walruses, sea otters and penguins, which was a feature of the last century, has been severely curbed, it has not been stopped. As recently as 1972 it was necessary to introduce international legislation to prevent the polar bear from being exterminated by sportsmen using helicopters.

Modern man, as the super-predator, conforms to none of nature's self-regulating laws. To serve his own interests, to gain wealth, or simply for self-indulgence, he has destroyed for ever many unique forms of life which were the end products of millions of years of evolution. Nothing can ever restore them and the world is a poorer place without them. Yet the fascination of killing remains. This was typified in a recent television interview with a wealthy American sportsman, who, having stated that he had spent $350,000 on shooting wild animals in every continent, declared that his next ambition was to kill a Siberian Tiger. There are only 130 of these magnificent animals left in the whole world. This fact has been widely publicized throughout the western world and it is difficult to believe that he did not know it.

16 The Paradox of Tourism

On my first visit to Africa, some thirty years ago, I already knew that something like ninety per cent of the populations of wild animals had disappeared since the days of Livingstone. Nevertheless, during the three days which my small, low-flying aircraft took to span the continent from what was then called the Gold Coast, across French Equatorial Africa and the Sudan to Eritrea, animals appeared to be still plentiful. Today's tourists, who are able to see half a million wildebeests migrating across the Serengeti plains in Tanzania, may find it hard to believe that they represent only a minute fraction of Africa's once incredibly abundant fauna. In fact, the tourist circuit of well-populated game reserves gives a very misleading impression of the appalling losses which have occurred during the past century. A number of species which even only fifty years ago were common have been completely wiped out and many more are now very rare. Had it not been for the strenuous efforts of the dedicated pioneer conservationists, most of Africa's larger animals would by now have vanished altogether.

The creation of the wildlife reserves in Africa, which today attract millions of tourists from all over the world, was a remarkable achievement. Few of those involved in such an act of faith could have foreseen the extent to which their efforts would be rewarded. The turning-point for African wildlife was the Arusha Declaration of 1961. Stimulated by the eloquence of Sir Julian Huxley, Sir Frank Fraser Darling and other world leaders in conservation, Prime Minister Nyerere of Tanganyika (now Tanzania) then made the first public commitment by any government to conserve wildlife as a national heritage for the benefit of posterity. The repercussions of this declaration and of the report on the conference published by UNESCO echoed around the world. The fears that once independence was restored to the African states the newly created wildlife reserves would be abandoned, as mere devices for the white man's pleasure, were speedily dispelled. Indeed, since that time the number of reserves has constantly been increased.

A dramatic indication of the regard in which some Africans hold their responsibilities to wildlife, was the fact that during the Congolese rebellion a number of game wardens in the Parc National Albert, although for a long period unpaid, stayed at their posts and were killed by rebels while defending the animals. Many Africans are now prominent members of international organizations concerned with conservation. Educational visits to reserves by parties of African schoolchildren are heartwarming indications that Africans really are beginning to regard their natural heritage as their own possession, in which they can rightly take pride.

None who attended the Arusha conference could have foretold the extraordinary growth of the African tourist industry which followed. The wildlife reserves and national parks, which had been created primarily to protect the endangered animals and scenic splendours of the continent, suddenly became major sources of much-needed foreign currency. In 1972 Kenya alone earned £18 million from people who came to enjoy the spectacle of lions, giraffes and elephants roaming unmolested among the umbrella-shaped acacias and yellow-barked fever trees of their natural habitat. This rapidly increasing revenue represents the strongest safeguard against the constant threat in some African States that reserves might be turned over to tribal settlement or cultivation.

The economic bonanza has, however, created new problems which are daily becoming more apparent. The time when one could drive all day in an African game reserve without seeing another vehicle are gone for ever. It is now almost impossible to photograph a lion without also including the ring of zebra-striped Land-Rovers which inevitably surrounds it. The density of vehicles within twenty miles of every tourist lodge is destroying the very thing which tourists are paying their millions to see — the sight of nature unsullied by human interference. As the crowds increase, so do regimentation, litter, noise and the number of buildings and roads. Towering, American-style skyscrapers now form the immediate background to the once isolated and scenically beautiful Nairobi National Park.

Wildlife tours have become a mixed blessing. They provide valuable income and local employment and play a major role in educating people to appreciate the wonders of the natural world. But the best behaved tourists cannot avoid causing some disturbance to wildlife, particularly during the breeding season. Vehicles damage the vegetation, dropped cigarettes cause fires and even an isolated pedestrian can introduce alien seeds on his clothing, which can eventually upset the natural ecology of a reserve.

These problems are greatly magnified when large tourist groups visit isolated islands, which over the millennia have evolved their own unique and hyper-sensitive ecosystems and endemic species of animals, plants, or invertebrates. Here the least disturbance or foreign introduction can have a disastrous consequence which, while perhaps negligible to the layman, can represent an irreparable loss to science. Many of the world's rarest creatures now survive in minuscule numbers only on single islands, which until now have escaped serious disturbance by man.

Unfortunately the lure of being able to advertise visits to a 'desert island paradise' is irresistible to the tourist trade, whose complete exploitation of traditional seaside playgrounds such as the Mediterranean or the Caribbean now leaves no further scope for expansion. The process of fringing the African coasts with high-rise hotels and holiday camps has already begun on a massive scale. It was inevitable that the off-shore and oceanic islands would also be embraced.

The speed with which the hitherto untouched Seychelles archipelago in the Indian Ocean was 'developed' for tourism shocked conservationists. Fortunately the Vallée de Mai

Reserve on Praslin Island already protected the giant *coco-de-mer* palms, which grow wild in no other part of the world. Cousin Island and its ultra-rare birds had also been saved, by the International Council for Bird Preservation. Since then, thanks to the efforts of Miss Phyllis Barclay-Smith, Sir Peter Scott, Christopher Cadbury and others, a crash programme of conservation has been undertaken. Varying degrees of protection have been given to Frigate Island and its unique magpie-robins, to Aride Island, to La Digue and its equally unique paradise flycatchers and to Bird Island and its two million sooty and noddy terns (*see* Plate 13). A marine national park now protects the endangered tropical fish and coral reefs around Mahé. On Mahé itself, the habitat of the world's rarest owl, the tiny bare-legged scops, is also a reserve.

I count myself fortunate to have seen the Seychelles before the jumbo-jet airport was built on Mahé—and to have been only the fourth man living to have set eyes on the almost legendary bare-legged scops owl. Since then tourists have swarmed in to occupy the hotels which have sprung up like mushrooms all along the enchantingly beautiful palm-fringed shores. Mahé is now in danger of becoming just another Jamaica. Doubtless before long the adjacent Amirante archipelago will also be exploited by the ever-hungry 'developers'.

Nothing is going to halt the growth of tourism. Rich or poor, every country seeks its economic rewards. The hardest lesson for any government to learn is that there are definite limits to carrying capacity. Few, if any, have yet shown much interest or skill in even trying to estimate this capacity in relation to the resources of an environment. A small country such as Great Britain, which contrives to squeeze 56 million people into its 96,500 square miles (a population density of well over 500 to the square mile) attracted no fewer than 7 million foreign tourists in 1972. At a conference of the British Travel Association it was stated that twice this number would be welcome. There was visible indignation when I pointed out that most of our holiday resorts and historic sites had already reached the point of self-destruction by the crowds they attracted, and that every new holiday camp or mile of motorway deprived our future generations of the peace and beauty of the countryside on which their well-being would depend.

Most environmental planners are aware of the price to be paid for a booming tourist industry, but their voices are shouted down by the economists and politicians who worship at the shrine of Gross National Product. Money comes first, the quality of life second. Every country accepts all the negative aspects of unlimited tourist development rather than forego the revenue it brings. Communist as well as Capitalist countries alike share this attitude. The wonderful sand beaches of the Black Sea in Bulgaria and the picturesque coasts of the Adriatic in Jugoslavia are rapidly being converted into sprawling masses of ugly hotels and holiday camps, thus destroying the natural environments which originally attracted tourists. Yet many people besides conservationists are deeply disquieted by the excesses to which this development so easily leads. The people of Spain, Hawaii, or Bali are certainly not proud of what they have encouraged foreign developers to do to the once beautiful shores of the Costa Brava, Waikiki and Sanur, any more than my own countrymen accept without bitter complaint the increasing ugliness and overcrowding of the now almost completely 'developed' south coast of England.

Yet although the average man dislikes overcrowding and the replacement of an unspoilt shore-line by high-rise hotels, we ourselves are part of the problem the moment we set foot on an aircraft or ship as tourists. While in our own country vehemently criticizing the behaviour of foreign tourists, we are often completely insensitive to the impression of our own mores abroad when the roles are reversed. The English tourist who complains noisily if he cannot get eggs and bacon for breakfast in Marrakesh, or the American matron who storms the hotel manager's office in Rawalpindi because there are no Kleenex tissues in her bathroom, are merely reflecting the belief of the western tourist that his or her domestic standards should be universal. These standards are, however, sometimes extremely harmful to the regard in which the western democracies, who form the great majority of tourism, are held by the poorer nations. Take the prying eye of the tourist's inevitable camera. Nearly all western tourists have been brought up to believe that everything seen can also be photographed. But many primitive peoples regard a camera lens as an evil eye which brings misfortune, or takes away part of themselves. A Balinese girl in dancing regalia does not mind being photographed during her performance because she is then looking her best; she objects strongly, however, if a tourist snaps her in working clothes in her native village. To photograph a bedouin woman is to risk being stoned or even knifed by her husband. Tourist photographers who clamber about in Hindu or Muslim temples or mosques while a religious ceremony is in progress in order 'to get a better shot' cause great offence, as do those who insist on trying to take 'close-ups' of the faces of people in almost any country. Yet such examples of embarrassing behaviour can be seen again and again on one's travels.

When Kathmandu became the Mecca of the hippies of the western world, the Nepalese, who hitherto had looked up to tourists as rather superior and very welcome visitors, had good reason to change their minds. Many of the hippies from rich families in the United States, Britain and western Europe, begged in the streets, or became prostitutes, in order to obtain money for drugs. Many of them eventually died in the dark alleys of the Kathmandu slums. The spectacle so outraged local public opinion that today no western tourist can enter Nepal without showing that he has sufficient funds to support himself.

A similar example of harm done to western prestige was the initiative of a German tourist company, which organized the notorious 'sex safaris' to Africa. Can one wonder that not every African today greets the tourist with a welcoming smile?

Almost no remote part of the world is now inaccessible to tourists. There are organized tours to the Gobi Desert, to the Russian Pamirs, to the Micronesian islands, to the uttermost parts of the Sahara and to the Arctic and Antarctic. Wherever the tourists go, there is a trail of Kodak cartons, Coca-Cola bottles, beer cans and cigarette packages. As each chattering group lands on a remote island, the ship's crew dumps over-board the tin cans, bottles, empty cartons and accumulated rubbish of the voyage, which presently drifts ashore to pollute the once pristine beaches. Every monument and sacred shrine will soon bear its quota of modern graffiti, enthusiastically scratched or painted by Elmer from Texas, Bert from Black-pool, or Hans from Frankfurt. I counted nearly one hundred such painted inscriptions on the rocks of the Galápagos Islands alone — some of which were thirty feet wide.

Soon all the adorable naked children of the Pacific and Indian Ocean islands in the sun will have learned to cup their hands and say the magic words, 'money, cigarettes, candy,' which since the last war must be the most universally repeated of any in the English language. In the wake of the tourists will come the 'developers', with their giant bulldozers and concrete-mixers. And after them will spring up the hotels and the rash of billboards advertising the gadgets and accessories without which the modern tourist is soon unhappy. Inventive entrepreneurs will emerge to exploit the demand for souvenirs, by selling locally trapped birds, feather or butterfly-wing ornaments, orchids, sea-shells, corals, tribal ornaments, or archaeological relics. Presently, when the island has been stripped of its native treasures, the entrepreneur will import the mass-produced souvenirs with which Hong Kong has swamped the world. Unique customs and costumes evolved during centuries of the island's history will gradually be abandoned in favour of imitations of their modern western counterparts. After the island has been sufficiently westernized to resemble Ibiza, Guam or Capri, it will cease to be advertised as an 'island paradise' and will be merely another place of call in the tour itineraries. A few of the islanders will have acquired wealth, others will have lost both land and livelihood. And the island will have lost its soul.

The exploitation of primitive communities has in recent years taken a more highly organized and sinister form. The demand for archaeological treasure and tribal artefacts has become big business. The robbing of Inca burial ground of their gold ornaments has reached such a scale that the Peruvian

Government has become thoroughly alarmed. The superb tribal masks and wood carvings of the New Guinea highlands and the Sepik River now command such astronomical prices in the art galleries of the world that almost no originals now remain in the island. In 1961 Michael Rockefeller alone collected some 500 carved shields, drums, paddles, canoe prows, ancestral figures, masks and other early Asmat (West Irian) artefacts for the New York Museum of Primitive Art. Though this collection was not made for personal gain (and he was unfortunately drowned while leaving the area), its value to anthropologists and as a public exhibit cannot be said to outweigh so great a loss to the culture of a small but still living civilization. The growing tendency for collectors, not only of such artefacts but also of ultra-rare birds, butterflies and plants, to say 'they will disappear anyway if I do not collect them' seems to me ethically indefensible. Equally questionable is the tourist literature which promises access to archaeological and native treasures which can be sold back home at ten or twenty times their purchase price. Tourism for mere pleasure, or for new experience, is giving way to tourism for personal profit.

Projecting this development into the twenty-first century, one can foresee the time when all the original native art will be in the hands of museums or private collectors. Tourists will then have to be content with the spectacle of primitive people wearing plastic imitations of their former head-dresses and ornaments. This time is not far off. Already in many parts of South America and Asia, gaudy plastic flowers and plastic models of local treasures are on sale. One of my saddest experiences was being greeted recently in Nepal with a horrible garland of plastic flowers, instead of the traditional garland of wild marigolds. In India and Pakistan tinsel is replacing garland flowers.

Of course there are tourist companies and tourists who are not insensitive to the consequences of the present developments. Indeed some tourist literature already speaks of 'last chances to see' primitive peoples and native art before they are engulfed in modernization. Some tourist companies are also scrupulous in controlling litter. However, the cheap 'package tour' operator, whose only concern is profit, takes no such precautions and has become a major threat not only to the preservation of primitive communities, but also to the natural ecosystems of many remote parts of the world.

The International Union for Conservation of Nature and Natural Resources is now pressing for an internationally accepted code of conduct for tourism and for the control of visits to places of particular scientific value. This may help to curb excesses, but it cannot reverse harm already done, nor replace lost treasures, either man-made or natural. Meanwhile, the syndrome of the disease of uncontrolled tourism continues unabated. It demonstrates its ultimate climax in the creation of whole cities expressly for the exploitation of tourists, such as one sees in the overwhelming vulgarity of Las Vegas, in Nevada. I would, however, rather see a dozen such tourist cities built in the countries which enjoy them, than impose the ugliness of western materialism on the few countries which still retain their innocence. International tourism may enlarge the enjoyment of the western world and swell the coffers of the recipient countries; but to those with eyes to see its fatal impact, it is a deeply disturbing paradox.

17 Operation Tiger

No conservation project in which I have been involved has given me greater personal satisfaction than the international effort which was made to save the tiger from extinction. Having studied tigers in the wild, I regard them as the most magnificent of all animals (*see* Plate 15). It was unthinkable to me that they should be allowed to disappear completely without a major effort being made to save them. 'Operation Tiger', as I called the project, became a personal crusade, on which I concentrated all my attention for the best part of two years.

I have mentioned in Chapter 10 the reasons for the disastrous decline of the tiger. When Operation Tiger was launched in 1972, the combined populations of all eight races of the species had dropped from about 100,000 in 1920 to barely 5,000. The Balinese race was already extinct; the Javan and Caspian races down to five and fifteen respectively; the Siberian, Chinese and Sumatran were in the very low hundreds. The Indo-Chinese race was rapidly being wiped out except in Malaya, which had only 600. Only the Indian race, of which perhaps 2,300 survived in India, Bangladesh, Nepal, Bhutan and western Burma, appeared to offer any hope for a successful rescue attempt. Already, however, there were few, if any, groups of the Indian race, which was scattered over an area two-thirds the size of Europe, large enough to represent a genetically viable breeding population. Unless protected reserves of sufficient size and with a sufficiency of prey species could be created to support contiguous populations of at least 100 tigers in each, the Indian race was also doomed. Unlike lions, which are rather sedentary and live in large family groups, tigers require large hunting areas and are solitary. The prospect of finding reserves of sufficient size, in countries already heavily over-populated with land-hungry humans, looked very remote.

These and many other difficulties were all too obvious to my scientific colleagues at the joint meeting of the I.U.C.N. and W.W.F., before whom I laid my proposals for Operation Tiger. Understandably, the W.W.F., whose income from voluntary contributions is always inadequate to meet the urgent demands which flow in from every country, was startled by my proposed budget of £400,000 for technical equipment, training, research and public education in the countries where the reserves were to be created. A large back-log of approved projects awaiting funds ruled out any possibility of financing my plans from existing resources.

With as much eloquence as I could summon, I pleaded that a delay of even one year would reduce the number of surviving tigers to a level which could well make the difference between success and failure. It was finally agreed that, subject to my obtaining the active co-operation of the governments concerned, the twenty National Appeals of the W.W.F. would mount a special fund-raising campaign. I was confident that the gloomy forecast of five years to raise the sum needed would be speedily disproved. Ten days later I was on my way to India.

My good friend Zafar Futehally, who represents both the I.U.C.N. and the W.W.F. in India, had organized a full programme for me in New Delhi. On the day of my arrival the leading newspaper carried a half-page advertisement describing the plight of the tiger and inviting attendance at a meeting at which Dr Karan Singh, Minister for Tourism and Civil Aviation and Chairman of the Indian Board for Wildlife, was to preside and at which I was to speak. Karan Singh, erstwhile Maharaja of Kashmir, is one of the outstanding political figures in India and a brilliant orator. The success of Operation Tiger largely depended on his personal interest in its implementation. He made this interest abundantly clear at the meeting and gave me very generous support. We had front

15. In the 1920s there were still 100,000 tigers in Asia. Barely 5,000 now remain, scattered in small groups between Siberia and Sumatra. India has only 1,827. The Balinese race is extinct, the Javan and Caspian races on the brink of extinction. The exploitation of forests, excessive hunting and the fur traders have caused these appalling losses.

16. Hundreds of thousands of square miles of the great rain forests in South America, Africa and Asia are being clear-felled or burnt. They represent the richest ecosystem on earth and the greatest store-house of evolutionary diversity. Once the fragile top-soil is exposed, the organic matter is oxidized and quickly eroded by the tropical rain.

page coverage in all the dailies next morning and I was invited to speak on radio and television.

I had long wanted to meet Prime Minister Indira Gandhi. This ambition was now fulfilled. In the course of my work I had met a number of Heads of State and other important personages, but never a woman Prime Minister, let alone one who successfully carried the appalling burden of leading a nation of 560 million people divided by acute differences in language, religion and caste structure. Her occasional appearances on B.B.C. television had given me an impression of her formidable intellect and extraordinary poise under the merciless cross-questioning to which our television interrogators now subject visiting dignitaries. To meet her informally in her quietly elegant study was a memorable experience.

To my surprise, she had seen my appearance on television the previous evening and was already aware of my views about the tiger, of which she fully approved. Her interest in wildlife was no mere pose. From her father Jawaharlal Nehru, the great crusader for India's freedom, she had inherited an abiding love of animals and a deep concern for the survival of her country's incomparable riches in wildlife. Her realistic approach to the problems of conservation in relation to the future of man had been demonstrated in a remarkable speech at the recent Stockholm Conference on the Environment. I had heard it described as the most constructive contribution of any made at this multi-national symposium.

I did not have to 'sell' my proposals for the creation of special reserves to Mrs Gandhi and she seemed quite unimpressed by the difficulties. Indeed, though she was pleased by the prospect of financial and scientific assistance from the W.W.F. and the I.U.C.N., she seemed confident that India could shoulder the major burden. The phrase 'India must stand on her own feet' had often occurred in her political speeches and was the source of a growing nationalistic pride, which occasionally rebuffed those who were genuinely anxious to help India. However, realizing that Operation Tiger could only succeed as the result of local initiative, I was only too pleased by her assurance.

12

Some of my Indian friends, long versed in the convolutions of domestic political procedures, had prophesied that the competing interests in land use by the various ministries, at both Central and State government levels, would lead to interminable delays before the tiger reserves could be created. I touched on this problem and suggested tentatively that strong co-ordination under her personal authority would seem to be required. Instantly the Prime Minister's sensitivity to political realities reacted. With what I can only describe as a sudden change from very feminine charm to rugged masculine decisiveness, she declared that a special committee, 'a tiger task force', would be formed and that it would be required to report to her personally. Greatly daring, I asked whether I might mention this important decision at my press conference that evening, to which she readily agreed.

To my later astonishment, the committee was formed next day, under the dynamic chairmanship of Dr Karan Singh. Dr K. S. Sankhala was appointed Director of the project and within a few months produced an admirably documented report and recommendations. No fewer than nine of India's best existing reserves, offering the optimum conditions for the long-term survival of the tiger, were listed for improvement and enlargement. The proposed budget, to be spread over the next six years, was the equivalent of nearly £2 million. The contribution which I had promised on behalf of the World Wildlife Fund was, of course, additional to this huge sum and was to be used for equipping the reserves to the required standards of scientific management and protection. With the Prime Minister's personal support, the Indian element of Operation Tiger obtained quick approval by the government and work on the reserves began in April 1973. It was the largest conservation project for wildlife ever mounted in Asia. When one recalls the tremendous domestic problems of India, no praise can be too high for the initiative and determination of the Tiger Task Force committee.

From India I moved to Bangladesh, then emerging from the horrors of the war, from which, with India's help, it had gained independence from Pakistan. I had made many Bengali friends at the time of my expeditions of 1966 and 1967 and looked forward to meeting those who had survived.

Entry to Bangladesh was still restricted to a daily flight from Calcutta to Dacca. On arrival at Calcutta I learned that the airline pilots had called a strike which might last for several days. As the first of a series of meetings in Dacca was scheduled for that afternoon, I decided to try to hitch a ride on one of the United Nations freight planes which were still ferrying food and medical supplies to the refugees in Bangladesh. There was an imposing row of big Russian helicopters loading on the tarmac, but I doubted that any of the pilots spoke English. A Swedish Red Cross freighter looked more promising. Its smiling, blond pilot obligingly agreed to find room for me among the seven tons of tins of biscuits which were already roped inside the aircraft. Without any of the tedious formalities of normal embarkation, I simply climbed aboard and we were off. I sat with several young Red Cross workers in the tail section.

As we crossed the well-remembered labyrinth of the Sunderbans swamps, the sky darkened with the inky and solid-looking cumulus clouds of a pre-monsoon storm. The moment we entered them, violent turbulence began to buffet the heavily laden aircraft. Lightning flashes became increasingly frequent. To escape the buffeting the pilot descended to 800 feet, but even at this altitude the plane was thrown about in an alarming manner, the wings flexing and shuddering as though smitten by a giant fist. The cargo began to break loose and the grinning co-pilot lurched along the swaying cabin to secure the ropes. Everything not securely attached was flying about and I was struck on the head by an air-borne thermos flask, which was fortunately empty. A sudden drop into a vacuum in the clouds threw me against my seat so violently that the back collapsed entirely and I was left hanging on to the arms for support. To calm my nerves I began timing the lightning flashes, which showed a rate of thirty-one to the minute. It was the worst electrical storm I had ever experienced. Having survived two rather exciting emergency landings during the War, I am fatalistic about flying, but I was more than thankful when we landed safely at Dacca.

'A bit bumpy, I'm afraid,' apologized the obliging Swedish pilot, as we shook hands on parting.

The bomb craters at the airport and along the highway to the city had merely been filled in with rubble; many of the buildings still bore the ugly scars of war. The Hotel International was, however, still functioning, though at much reduced standards. I took a hasty shower and hurried, an hour late, to my first appointment.

To re-enter a much-loved country from which one has been separated by war is a disturbing experience, in which anxiety, reunion, sorrow and relief become rapidly intermingled. In Dacca there was much to remind me of the emotions I had experienced as a soldier, when I re-entered liberated Paris in 1944, after having lived there for some years before the War. The same fear of enquiring the whereabouts of friends who might not have survived.

The indefatigable Karim, who had been the mainstay of my earlier explorations of the Sunderbans and Hill Tracts, was in Dacca to greet me and as eager as ever to forward the cause of conservation. My old friend Nuruddin Ahmad, now Secretary for Agriculture, welcomed me with open arms. Angus Hume, the expatriot Scots colonel, who knew more about the birds of Bangladesh than any of us, had also survived, though a bullet fired through his window was still buried in his dining-room wall.

At a formal meeting at the Ministry of Forests I heard with relief that the detailed recommendations on conservation which I had made to the old régime had been adopted as the official programme by the new Bangladesh Government. The war had caused little disturbance to the Sunderbans, because there were no roads and almost no human habitations in the region. This still held first priority as a national park site and was still believed to contain about one hundred tigers — probably the largest remaining single concentration left in Asia. My proposal that the area should come within the scope of Operation Tiger was enthusiastically agreed. Help in planning the management and protection of the Sunderbans was urgently needed, but, unlike India, Bangladesh had neither the qualified manpower nor the financial resources to import specialists for this work. I promised the Minister, Sohrab Hossain, that help would be forthcoming.

I was taken to meet General Osmani, the hero of the Bangladesh Army, who was still in the military hospital recovering from exhaustion and malnutrition. This splendid soldier was President of the newly formed Bangladesh Wildlife Preservation Society and, to the distraction of the doctors and nurses, was directing its work with enthusiasm from his sick-bed. His telephone interrupted our discussion frequently.

My next call was on the President of Bangladesh, Justice Abu Syed Choudhury. After an hour's wide-ranging discussion, I was captivated by his courtly charm and by the detached, philosophical manner in which he was able to view the turbulent birth of the new nation. As we parted, he said rather sadly that the beauties of nature were one of the few assets to survive the war. The help of the World Wildlife Fund in continuing their preservation and in making the public aware of them would be deeply appreciated as a contribution to the reconstruction of a peaceful existence.

The contrast between this leisurely discussion with the President and my meeting with Prime Minister Sheikh Mujibur Rahman later that evening could scarcely have been greater. I was accompanied by Karim and Angus Hume. The building where the P.M. worked every day from early morning until the small hours of the night, was heavily guarded. Once past the sentries, we had to push our way through a milling throng of officials, journalists and petitioners, who crowded every inch of the ground floor and the stairway to the ministerial offices above. Press photographers were playing with a young leopard which someone had just presented to the Prime Minister. We were served with the inevitable tea, but had scarcely tasted it before he burst into the room, greeting us with complete informality. His secretary had warned us that he would be in a hurry. 'He is always in a hurry,' he added, rather despairingly.

Sheikh Mujibur Rahman radiated vitality and nervous energy. While we talked, he was in almost constant motion, sitting first on the sofa beside me, then on the table, or striding up and down the room. As briefly as I could, I outlined the purpose of my visit and the conclusions reached at the various meetings. He welcomed the interest of the World Wildlife Fund in Bangladesh and said that the development of the Sunderbans as a national park was just what he wished. Foreign currency was badly needed and tourism was the quickest way of obtaining it. As he warmed to this theme, his face lit up and from then on he did most of the talking. The wildlife of Bangladesh would be part of the reconstruction plan for the country, he said. Everything and everyone was needed to get the country back on its feet.

'Conservation is certainly part of my plan,' he declared. 'The destruction of our forests has been terrible. Thousands of tons of the best timber were taken every year by Pakistan and what remained has been badly damaged by the war. With hundreds of villages destroyed, we are now very short of timber for building and of sungrass for thatching. But do you know what I did? Two days after becoming Prime Minister I issued a decree forbidding the felling of any more trees for five years and forbidding the killing of any more wild animals! India has promised to help us and we will import timber and sungrass until ours has recovered. The tiger? Why, it's now our national emblem and is the watermark on our banknotes! Of course we shall protect the tiger.'

His enthusiasm was wonderful. He was a man accustomed to dramatic speech and dramatic action — a man larger than life. I began to understand that only such a man could have broken through the centuries-old apathy of the patient Bengali peasants and led them through a fratricidal struggle to create a new nation.

He began talking about the Chittagong Hill Tracts, where the Indian Army was still mopping up pockets of resistance. 'We must have a great national park there,' he said. 'There are still plenty of tigers and elephants in those forests — and a wonderful lake which thousands of western tourists would enjoy.'

I had not the heart to disillusion him about the tigers, which had disappeared soon after the Kaptai Dam had been built in their best area. But I knew that Karim longed to develop the plan I had put forward in 1966 for converting the Pablakhali Reserve at the head of the Kaptai Lake into a much larger national park. Even without its tigers it would still be a very attractive proposition, because of its remarkably abundant bird life and superb riverine forests. I had good reason to remember Pablakhali, because it was there that Eric Hosking and I were charged by two bull gayals (a race of the gaur jungle bison) which we were photographing. One does not forget such an experience easily.

I left the Prime Minister's office aware that I had not been able to discuss all the details of Operation Tiger. However, Karim seemed delighted by our having been accorded so long an interview by a man who lived by the minute.

It was after nine o'clock and I was feeling very tired after averaging four meetings a day for eight days. However, I did my best to enthuse the waiting press correspondents with our plans for Operation Tiger in Bangladesh. When they had finished asking questions, I was handed a microphone and asked to record a summary for the local radio station. I did so against a background of honking taxi horns and chatter which must have rendered it almost unintelligible.

Angus saw me off to Kathmandu early the following morning and handed me a bunch of clippings arising from the press conference. He will be sadly missed in Bangladesh now that he has returned to his native Scotland.

John Blower, who has done so much for conservation in East Africa and Nepal, met me at Kathmandu airport. With him I was surprised to see George Schaller, whom I had last met when he was completing his remarkable study of snow leopards in Chitral, at the other end of the Himalayas. He had become an almost legendary figure to the hill tribesmen, who were ready to swear that he had been seen walking in the snow with snow leopards trotting along on either side of him. He was now waiting for a plane back to Pakistan, after completing a study of the high altitude sheep and goats of the Nepalese

Himalayas. In the half hour before his plane arrived, we three had much news to exchange.

My few days in Nepal were not at all strenuous. H.M. King Birendra was unfortunately still in mourning for his father and very preoccupied with matters of State, so I was unable to see him. I therefore had time between other official meetings to make two enjoyable field trips. The first was to the Chitawan reserve, where I wanted to check up on the status of the tigers, which had increased to twenty. There were at least as many in the Sukla Phanta Reserve in western Nepal. One of the objects of my negotiations was to try to obtain the much more valuable Karnali Royal Hunting Preserve for Operation Tiger. King Mahendra had promised to consider converting it into a protected reserve the last time I had met him. I am glad to say that since then the king has confirmed its new status. It is now the best tiger reserve in the country.

The second trip, which I also made by light plane by the kindness of the local United Nations office, was to Langtang, where John Blower was hoping to create a Himalayan national park. It is a spectacular region of high peaks on the Tibetan border above the Trisuli watershed and includes the beautiful Gosainkund lakes, at 14,000 feet above sea level. Our approach, weaving among the snow-clad mountains, was breath-taking as each new vista unrolled before us. We landed bumpily in the trough of a small, enclosed valley of stony ground at 12,400 feet, just below the towering mass of Mount Langtang. An avalanche of shining snow was thundering down its slope as we landed. A herd of shaggy yaks trotted away—they probably belonged to one of the Buddhist monasteries. Above us, Himalayan griffon vultures, lammergeiers and alpine choughs were wheeling; beneath our feet was a carpet of miniature gentians and saxifrages. Obviously it was a wonderful site for a national park (*see* Plate 5).

The only problem lay in the recent settlement of a large group of Tibetan Khambas in the very centre of the proposed national park site. These para-military refugees were credited with having effected the escape of the Dalai Lama from the Chinese Army and had been given sanctuary by Nepal. Why they should have been settled in an area which for years had been discussed as the site for a national park remained a mystery. According to all accounts they were heavily armed and spent most of their time killing off all the blue sheep, gorals, bears and other wildlife in the region.

I discussed this problem later with several officials and with the king's secretary, urging that the Khambas should be settled elsewhere, before they wiped out every animal in the area. The replies were somewhat evasive: I was told that any action which might be construed as persecution of the saviours of the Dalai Lama would cause great offence to public opinion, not only in Nepal but in other countries. My suggestion that resettlement in a more fertile and less remote valley could scarcely be regarded as persecution, fell on deaf ears. There was evidently more to the Khambas than met the eye of a stranger. The mystery was heightened for me by persistent rumours that they had been seen to receive a parachute drop of arms and supplies from a C.I.A. plane operating from Taiwan. A very picturesque touch, though it was apparently taken quite seriously in Kathmandu.

Since my visit, plans are still going forward for the Langtang national park. I hope they will succeed, though I cannot imagine that many tourists will want to get too near the trigger-happy Khambas, if they are allowed to remain there.

An even more important development was announced in Bonn at the 1973 World Wildlife Congress by H.R.H. Prince Gyanendra, who is now in charge of conservation in Nepal. Mount Everest and 480 square miles of the upper Khumbu region around it were to become a national park. As John Blower and I had for years been discussing this possibility, almost as a utopian dream, I was overjoyed. The region is of incomparable scenic magnificence and of unique value to science. In recent years both the uncontrolled exploitation of the blue pine, fir, juniper and rhododendron forests and the rapid increase in uncontrolled tourist visits were causing grave concern. By turning the area into a national park, these threats could be brought under control and both the vegetation and the wildlife which are dependent upon it could be given effective protection. Yet, on reflection, I began to feel uneasy about the announcement.

Few ecosystems are as vulnerable as those of high mountains. The wildlife and alpine plant communities have evolved under conditions of a rigorous environment. Because of their biological isolation, they have little leeway for survival or resistance to interference. Several distinguished British, German and Japanese botanists have studied the vegetation of the Khumbu in detail. John Blower and before him Graeme Caughley made inventories of the wildlife. Mammal species are less numerous than in the western Himalayas and none now exists in large populations. Nevertheless, they include rare species such as the snow leopard, black bear and red panda. The ungulates include the blue sheep, the Himalayan tahr, the goral, the serow and the much persecuted little musk deer. Birds include several important species of rare pheasants and the snow partridge and a host of colourful chats, finches, thrushes, tits and warblers. It is a rich though highly sensitive region.

Obviously it is proper that the world should have access to the glories of the Everest massif. But if these glories are to be not merely scenic and if the unique vegetation and wildlife are to survive, access must be very carefully controlled, otherwise the national park will be self-destroying. Without doubt, the Everest National Park could quickly become one of the greatest tourist attractions in the world and a very important factor in Nepal's economy. But herein lies the danger. If the lure of massive tourist revenue is allowed to outweigh sound conservation principles and the need for extremely thorough ecological planning, irreparable damage could be done. Present plans call for the construction of ten small rest-houses in the Khumbu, which, with the inclusion of the existing lodge near Khumjung (a private Japanese-Nepali venture) would provide simple accommodation for a total of 214 tourists, plus those who prefer tented camps. The number of tourists visiting the Khumbu has increased by five and a half times in the past three years. The creation of the national park and the provision of rest-houses could, and I suspect will, result in an immediate and very rapid increase in international tourism to Nepal. Already the marked increase in tree lopping and tree felling to provide fuel for tourist camps is alarming. So also is the increase in litter and garbage on the Khumbu trails. The new lodges are, very properly, to be constructed of materials procured outside the national park area, and steps are being taken to control the present degradation of the forests by the Sherpa villagers, who are dependent on wood for fuel and on rhododendrons for both winter fodder and bedding for their cattle.

However, the importation of fuel and fodder to the Sherpas who will have to service the new lodges and their trekking parties, and to supply food and other necessities for tourists, will inevitably increase the volume of traffic into the national park. The present plans have been admirably drawn to minimize these consequences, and to keep tourism within practical limits. But I fear that the tourist potential of the Khumbu has been under-estimated. The world's tourists are thirsting for new experiences. Most of them have 'done' the African game reserves and major tourists' sites of the world. How long will it be before the wealthy tour operators, airlines and property developers seize the opportunity to capitalize on the lure of Mount Everest? It will be only a short time before the big western consortiums offer to build large modern hotels in the Khumbu. If the Nepalese Government should rise to this bait, conservationists will have lost the battle to save the natural treasures of the Khumbu ecosystem.

Six months after my round of visits in India, Bangladesh and Nepal, I returned for further discussions. This time I also included the romantic little kingdom of Sikkim, though I fear there are very few tigers left there. Operation Tiger was by then making splendid progress. A total of fourteen special reserves were in preparation, nine in India, three in Nepal and one each in Bangladesh and Bhutan. The killing of tigers and the export of their skins is now banned in these countries and in several others also. India had just introduced legislation which would make it illegal for any shop or bazaar to hold tiger skins or offer them for sale, thus dealing a final heavy blow to those who supported the black market and always claimed that the skins they offered had been obtained before hunting was banned. Forty-three nations had signed a solemn agreement not to permit the importation of the skins of tigers, nor of a long list of other endangered species.* Throughout the world the press had supported our campaign. Three new books on the tiger had appeared (including one which I wrote for the W.W.F.), all drawing attention to Operation Tiger. Sixty-four of the world's airlines had agreed not to carry hunters intending to shoot endangered animals such as the tiger. Money had flowed in at a rate beyond expectations and, as this book goes to press, the half-way mark towards the target of £400,000 has already been passed in only nine months. The famous animal painter David Shepherd alone raised £100,000 by the gift of a superb portrait of a tiger, of which a limited edition of reproductions was snapped up by collectors in eight weeks.

My conviction has been vindicated that once civilized people were made aware of the danger of losing the best known and most beautiful of the world's wild animals, they would react positively. The crusade is far from won yet, but I am now increasingly confident that at the eleventh hour the Indian tiger will be saved for posterity.

Not the least gratifying aspect of this campaign was its effect on countries other than those directly concerned with the survival of the Indian race of the tiger. The Soviet Union, always active in conservation, had increased its efforts on behalf of the Siberian race, as had Malaya and Thailand for the Indo-Chinese race and Indonesia for the Sumatran and Javan races. Iran had undertaken an urgent study of the status of the Caspian tiger. Even more pleasing was a report that the Chinese Government, which had previously classified the Chinese tiger as vermin, was now giving it legal protection.

At the time of writing, Britain had not ratified it.

18 Life in the 21st Century

I suppose there has never been a time when thoughtful people have not had serious doubts about the future of the human race. Nor, indeed, when they did not sigh for the good old days, which in retrospect always seem more tranquil than the prospect of the immediate future. Perhaps there were exceptions, when hope illuminated men's minds, as it did with the advent of Christianity and during the Renaissance in Europe. But judging by history, each new generation seems to find more comfort from times remembered than from peering into the unknown.

Certainly today there is precious little comfort to be found in the inexorability of the computerized forecasts now being made about the world in which our grandchildren will live. Nothing in these calculations of exponential growth weighs more heavily upon us than the certainty of a rise in the human population from the present 3,632 million to 6,100 million in the next thirty years. Those who worry about the quality of the life we now lead may well shudder at such a prospect. The demographers assure us that, even if efforts to control the birth-rate are pressed to the maximum, there is little hope of equating births with deaths before the year 2050 and that the world's population may become stabilized around 2070 at a level of nearly 15,500 million — well over four times the present figure. The whites, who will achieve stability first, will then be a small minority in a world of browns, blacks and yellows. To illustrate this point, India's population is rising eight times faster than that of Great Britain.

Professor Arnold Toynbee, in his remarkable book *Cities on the Move*, forecasts for the twenty-first century a form of human settlement without precedent in history. He calls it 'Ecumenopolis', from the Greek *hé oikoumenë* — the inhabited earth. We can already see the first indications of his prophecy of 'world cities' coming true in the growth of London, New York, or Tokyo, by the insidious progress of what the town planners call 'in-filling' and the erosion of the protective green-belts. It is becoming apparent even to speculators that the social penalties for crowding people into enormous multi-storey dwellings are too serious for this solution to be acceptable. Plans for thousand-storey tenements to relieve the shortage of building land are therefore unlikely to be fulfilled. Cities will be forced to expand laterally.

Toynbee has shown that in all highly developed countries, science and technology have enabled agriculture and animal husbandry to produce far more and better quality food from fewer men employed per acre of land. Small farmers who are unable to keep up with this trend are forced to abandon their calling and move to the cities. In the poorer countries, on the other hand, it is the younger and more ambitious farmers who, recognizing that their type of farming cannot pay, are leaving the land to seek their fortunes in the cities. Neither of these displaced groups necessarily succeeds in the radical change to an urban environment, nor finds work there. Many farming families therefore swell the ranks of the unemployed and gravitate to the poorest districts, as can be seen in the ever-growing shanty-town area of, for example, Lima. Throughout most of the world this massive migration to the cities is apparent. Within a few generations from now, the overwhelming majority of mankind will be living in or around the fringes of cities of such mammoth proportions as will dwarf the largest of present-day conurbations. As the cities spread, they will engulf all the main centres of employment. Toynbee foresees not only that Boston, New York, Philadelphia, Baltimore and Washington will merge, but that they will ultimately link up with the Great Lakes complex of Chicago and Detroit. He foretells a similar linking-up of the major cities in Japan, Britain, western Europe and lowland Asia.

Fortunately for humanity, there are limits to the Ecumeno-polis theory. Though Toynbee is pessimistic, there is perhaps a faint hope that a universally acceptable solution may be found to the galloping birth-rate before we reach this stage. Second is the limiting factor of the availability of fresh water, which is already an acute problem in many countries. Although the desalinization of sea water appears to offer an obvious solution, the high cost of the process and of pumping it inland will greatly limit its development. The continental world-cities of the future may therefore have to be located near major lakes, whether man-made or natural. Few of the world's great rivers will by then be allowed to discharge their waters into the sea, but will be siphoned off for human use.

The control of pollution, which today is in its infancy, will become a major preoccupation of all governments and in-dustries. The present argument that pollution caused by old-fashioned blast furnaces or paper-mills must be suffered rather than cause unemployment, will not remain acceptable. The food sources of the oceans will be rigorously protected from pollution by the discharge of harmful effluents, including the dumping of radio-active atomic wastes, nerve gases and biological warfare stocks. The genetic consequences of today's pollution will by then be clearly measurable. It is unlikely that we shall tolerate, as we do now, the fact that the breast-milk of nursing mothers in the citrus valleys of California contains up to six times more DDT than is permitted by Federal law in human foods, or that people living near the pesticide factories in India hold the world record for the absorption of cancer-forming chemicals. Neither will chemical companies which find their products banned as too harmful in their own coun-tries be permitted, as they are now, to sell them to less sophis-ticated countries which are not yet fully aware of their dangers.

It is, of course, not mere commercial greed or wickedness, but failure to make use of ecological knowledge which is re-sponsible for most of the eco-catastrophes inflicted on the world by modern technology. Many of these catastrophes have originated in admirable intentions to improve the social or economic standards of needy people, under what Raymond

Dasmann and his colleagues* have called 'the development imperative'. The disastrous British government groundnut scheme in Tanzania was one such example. The mishandled Aswan Dam project by the Russians was another. The losses of wildlife, which represented valuable protein to the local tribes, during the flooding of the Kariba Dam in Rhodesia, and of valuable timber during the miscalculated flooding of the Kaptai Dam in Bangladesh, were equally serious. If a dam is desperately needed in an arid land and its construction results in a rapid spread of *bilharzia*, the deadly water-snail fever which is the scourge of the southern hemisphere, the local government may be willing to regard the consequences as less important than the lack of water and hydroelectric power. We cannot blame the decision makers if they are ready to pay a high price for social progress. Every country has the right to determine its own priorities for internal development. But we can and must make sure that, if we are involved, the price is known in advance. We must, however, also be willing to sympathize with the needy Indian worker in the fertilizer factory who says, 'I'd rather see pollution coming from a factory which provides employment than have no factory at all.' Our responsibility, if we provide the factory, is to minimize the harmful outcome.

One of the most rewarding results of discussions between the World Wildlife Fund and the World Bank was the decision that in future no major civil engineering project will be financed unless the ecological consequences have first been fully analysed and considered. The bank now has its own expert ecologists. Not only ecological damage but a tragic waste of money is involved when such projects fail. Work on the cross-Florida barge canal and on the proposed new international airport on the edge of the Everglades National Park was abandoned after conservationists had demonstrated the disastrous ecological consequences involved. Though not financed by the World Bank, these abortive projects cost the American taxpayers 63 million dollars.

* See *Ecological Principles for Economic Development* by Dasmann, Milton and Freeman, 1973. John Wiley & Sons Ltd. London.

Not all the prophets agree with Toynbee's gloomy but admirably reasoned forecasts. Escapists may comfort themselves by dismissing him as a prophet of doom, though many other scholars of international repute have sounded similar, if less closely argued, warnings. Even the optimists, however, now concede that within the lifetime of our children there will be twice the number of people to feed, house and educate. When one ponders the appalling conditions of over-crowding in which most of the citizens of, for example, Calcutta, now live, it is difficult to believe that such misery may be re-doubled. We in Britain are rightly indignant that several hundred homeless down-and-outs are still obliged to sleep on park benches or in the doorways of our capital city. But in Calcutta the number who do so every night of the year is already estimated at half a million. One can only hope that before India's 560 million population has doubled, the concept of the brotherhood of man will have deeper roots and that the United Nations will have become a more effective instrument in alleviating human suffering.

All the rich nations of the world are, to a greater or lesser degree, supporting the humanitarian work of the U.N. However, to judge these efforts in proper perspective, a balance must be struck between giving and taking. About eighty per cent of foreign aid has strings attached, in other words the recipient nations are expected to use it for the purchase of equipment, food or services from the donor nations. At the same time the donor nations erect tariff barriers against the exports of the poorer countries. Not only are the wealthy nations extracting by the exploitation of local resources, or through local manufacture, far more than they are putting back through Foreign Aid or local employment, they are also the chief degraders and polluters of the environments of the poorer countries through their mining, engineering, or industrial projects abroad. The richest nation, the United States, which has only $6\frac{1}{2}$ per cent of the world's population, consumes 40 per cent of all the available natural resources and is responsible, directly or indirectly, for 50 per cent of the earth's pollution. According to American sources, it produces four times more food calories than it needs, yet while most of its South American neighbours suffer from protein deficiency, the United States has taken thousands of tons of protein-rich anchovies from the off-shore waters of Peru for processing as food for its poultry or domestic cats. Similar behaviour is, of course, to be found among other highly developed countries, though only Americans are courageous enough to publish such criticisms of their own actions. Nevertheless, in a world in which one third of the inhabitants live at a bare subsistence level, it must be difficult for a hungry man to see the justification for the expenditure in 1972 of $1,260 million on pet foods in the United States.

Though the United States is by far the most generous benefactor to the hungry nations, and all the democracies are also giving substantial help, the hard fact remains that the gulf between the haves and the have-nots is continuing to widen. Only the emergence of a more realistic world conscience will enable this imbalance to be narrowed. Herman Kahn, in a recent United Nations publication, wrote: 'There is a sense in which altruistic aid can be more important to the rich than to the poor — essential for their own self-respect, for their own sense of worth, and perhaps to appease feelings of guilt.' The comments of Samir Amin, Director of the African Institute for Economic Development, were more harsh: 'Europocentrism and Americanocentrism account for an inability to conceive a future universal civilization other than one which fosters the extension of consumerismo to the privileged groups throughout the world.'

Meanwhile, philosophers among the poorer nations may well wonder whether the quality of life now enjoyed in the affluent societies, such as we see in the United States, Japan and western Europe, is any happier than their own. The negative aspects of our society are, of course, those which gain the widest attention abroad. Many leaders of the poorer countries are now questioning our assurances that only good can come from teaching the world to drink Coca-Cola, or to wish to possess an automobile. For our part, we are beginning to learn that we are creating aspirations which in many instances will be unattainable. Even amongst ourselves there are now many who are beginning to question the politicians and economists who keep repeating that the only yardstick for measuring national progress is an ever-increasing Gross National Product. This fallacious belief in perpetual growth from finite resources has been the cornerstone of the planning edifice since the beginning of the industrial revolution. We know now quite clearly that these resources are *not* inexhaustible. Man has been extracting minerals for 1,500 years, though he has been an industrialist for only 150. More than half of all the minerals ever extracted were taken in the last sixty years. Such a rate of exploitation obviously could not continue indefinitely and we are now told that many of the minerals essential to industry, such as lead, tin, zinc, copper and mercury, will be exhausted within the next thirty or so years. It has, of course, been known for many years that oil resources were running out. The energy crisis of 1973, which came as such a profound shock to the western world, was therefore not so difficult to foresee as politicians would have us believe. Its timing was merely advanced by Arab opportunism. Perhaps this will come to be regarded as a salutary lesson in focusing attention on the need to seek alternatives to our dwindling resources. But although modern technology may be capable of developing substitutes, the base materials for these must also be found in the earth.

I do not under-estimate the skills of human inventiveness in the face of the problems of the twenty-first century. The forward surge of man's progress has achieved many seeming miracles in the past and doubtless many a new genius will emerge from our great educational and research centres. But it would be a mistake to believe that new technology will provide all the solutions. Far more important will be the need for new political and social doctrines, based on the priorities for survival, in which progress can be measured not in materialistic terms, but in the quality of life sustainable in the face of increasing numbers and declining resources.

The hard arithmetic of survival beyond the twenty-first century will require a great measure of sacrifice by the richer nations. Not only will nationalistic principles have to be greatly modified, but the sacred cow of continued economic growth will have to be slaughtered. In order to survive, man must learn to live with, instead of against nature; to conserve instead of destroying or polluting the precious natural resources of the biosphere — the clean air, the fresh water, the oceans, the land, and the living organisms on which his very life depends. To recycle, instead of wasting, all materials used in manufacture. To abandon the theory of built-in obsolescence as a means of stimulating the demand for automobiles and household appliances and to build instead goods which will last. If man is to maintain his equilibrium in a crowded urban existence, he must exchange the tensions of a highly competitive society for one in which materialism is no longer admired. The alternative of attempting to maintain the present headlong course on which the developed countries are embarked, can only lead to a power struggle for control of the dwindling resources of the world, in which, in a nuclear age, there can be no winners.

Our greatest immediate problem is to induce politicians to admit that any crisis is impending. Very few of them, in any country, are willing to concern themselves with unpopular measures which cannot begin to bear fruit until long after their own likely terms of office have expired. Even fewer would be prepared to attempt to reverse the deeply rooted belief in continued economic growth to which they and all political parties are wedded. As national governments lack the means for global studies, there is in any event little likelihood that any one of them would take the lead in such a matter as this. The only existing forum which, at least on paper, should be appropriate for debating a strategy for the survival of the human race is the General Assembly of the United Nations. The record of this august body in tackling fundamental issues does not encourage optimism, however. To the anxious layman it appears chiefly as a forum for complaints over sovereignty, which divide rather than unite humanity. Moreover, the widespread lack of understanding of environmental and ecological principles among most of the world's politicians would seriously handicap debate. Nevertheless, a Select Committee, drawing on the now abundant resources of science, could be created to examine the evidence and to put it into a form comprehensible to the layman. There is perhaps in the General Assembly a hidden Wilberforce, a fearless crusader, who would brush aside the timorous and the supporters of vested interests, who would not rest until he had created by his eloquence a climate of opinion in which the necessary reforms could be introduced. I am perhaps naïve enough to hope this might be possible.

The publication in 1972 of a remarkable document entitled *A Blueprint for Survival* by *The Ecologist* magazine, represented the first attempt by a group of professional environmentalists to assess the evidence of the threats to the life-systems of our planet, and to formulate proposals for international action to prevent a final breakdown. It was courageous, unemotional and well documented. The world-wide demand for reprints indicated that an infinitely larger number of people were already deeply concerned about the future than either scientists or politicians could have imagined. Though neither all the opinions expressed, nor all the conclusions reached, in the *Blueprint* met with universal acceptance, it was widely applauded. No fewer than 187 scientists in Britain alone affirmed their support for action to be taken by the government, to formulate more effective policies to control the birthrate, to conserve and recycle resources, and to protect the environment. Moreover, they offered their services *en bloc* in devising these policies. There was no response from the government.

This stubborn political myopia is certainly not restricted to Britain. Time is not on our side. With every tick of the clock the human problems of the world become more difficult to overcome. Today 100 million children are suffering from severe protein deficiency. In spite of foreign aid, famine is rampant in many parts of Asia, Africa and South America. U.N. statistics show that among the 120 developing nations of the world, only 31 yet have policies favouring a lower rate of population growth. Yet while the world's human population is rising inexorably, the production of food is declining — and declining most rapidly in the poorer countries which need it most. Russia, China and South America used to be major exporters of food and are now importers. The much heralded 'green revolution' with its 'miracle rice' and 'wonder wheat' can only succeed where governments provide irrigation and heavy subsidies for the essential in-put of fertilizers. Some governments have shown that they would rather subsidize an airline, or build grandiose capital cities, than help their people to fend off starvation by improving the land for agriculture.

I cannot do better than quote the conclusion reached by the authors of the *Blueprint* in discussing these political realities: 'If we plan remedial action with our eyes on political rather than ecological reality, then very reasonably, very practicably, and very surely, we will muddle our way to extinction.'

I wonder whether any of the world's leaders read this simple statement. And, if so, whether they felt a slight twinge of conscience.

19 A Window on the World

One of the most fiercely resented impositions ever introduced in my over-taxed country was the window tax of 1696. Tax dodgers in those days were probably just as ingenious as they are today, though they ran greater risks as we have replaced mutilation and death for transgressors by mere fines or imprisonment. But the penalty the nation paid for the window tax can still be seen nearly three centuries after it was levied by the unloved William III, in the bricked-up windows of many of our ancient buildings. Every house was taxed at a flat rate of two shillings, plus a sliding scale of charges according to the number of its windows. The excuse that this was a temporary measure, to make good the budget deficiency caused by the then current practice of clipping silver coins, fooled nobody. In the first year the tax produced £1,200,000 — a prodigious sum in those days. As anticipated, it was increased six times during the succeeding century as more and more people bricked-up their windows. A minor reduction in 1823 failed to placate the long-suffering householders and finally, after violent agitation in the winter of 1850, the tax was repealed, only to be replaced by the ever more productive system for filling the national coffers to which we now submit.

I sometimes wonder whether the smallness of windows in most modern English houses is an unconscious reflection of William III's misguided tax, the memory of which was of course still fresh in the minds of the late Victorians. Or perhaps it merely reflects the Englishman's inherent desire for privacy — his dislike of being observed by his neighbours.

Small windows in city houses may be an advantage in shutting out the surrounding ugliness, but in the country there is surely every reason for them to be as large and as numerous as one's capacity to keep the rooms warm in winter will permit.

When my wife and I decided to build our house in Sussex, we chose a spot on a hill-top with a magnificent view, unimpeded to the south for a distance of twelve miles to the sea, which on a clear day peeps between the shoulders of the South Downs. On the skyline to the left rises Willingdon Hill and Bullock Down, from which the mighty cliff of Beachy Head juts out into the English Channel. Next on the right are the high contours of the Long Man and Windover Hill, reaching the sea in the white chalk precipices of the Seven Sisters. Then comes the Cuckmere Gap, its winding river fed from a stream rising from the lake in our valley. And to the right again, above the tiny village of Bopeep, is Firle Beacon, whose crest is 713 feet above sea level.

At the foot of our lawn is a deep ha-ha, enabling us to enjoy the sight of grazing cattle without the interruption of a visible fence. The meadow then falls away gently to the valley, where the big trees of Oxpasture Wood screen a placid lake beloved by wild ducks. On the other side of the wood the checkered farmlands rise and fall, so that in misty weather the higher coppices stand as disembodied sentinels in serried ranks above the whiteness. Half hidden in the valley, the peach-coloured stone gables of Possingworth Manor, which was rebuilt in 1657 during Cromwell's Commonwealth, are just visible. Near our house, sheltering it from the westerly gales, is a wood of noble beeches, through whose silvery trunks we watch the red sun setting during the winter solstice. By mid-summer the arc of the sun's position swings wider, to sink with dramatic precision between the silhouettes of our two most venerable park oaks. Even to the north the view is beautiful, a winding drive leading to a varied skyline of tall trees above banks of rhododendrons, azaleas and flowering cherries. Such a site as this cried out for windows large enough to let us enjoy the view at all seasons.

Thus it was that in every room of our house the windows

were stretched from wall to wall. To the consternation of the builder, who muttered forebodingly of wind pressures and unsupported beams, I insisted that the wide sweep of the southern view dictated an uninterrupted sheet of glass thirty feet wide by seven high. Although at that time so large a piece of plate glass had not yet been made in England, our picture window was eventually installed. It weighed more than a ton and, having been mercury-floated, is completely without distortion. Every day of the year it gives us joy.

Opposite the window we dug the modern equivalent of the Sussex dewponds which used to be such an attractive feature of the Downs. Our only concession to modern technology was to puddle the clay above a hidden lining of plastic sheeting in order to reduce drainage. Being on an exposed hill-top, it was an instant success with our local wildlife, which from dawn to dusk come to bathe or drink. In summer the water is starred with pink, white and yellow water-lilies. Around one side we planted a riot of dwarf Japanese azaleas, Siberian irises and kingcups, which add their reflections to the water. Occasionally a kingfisher delights us by dropping in to sample the goldfish and more than once a hungry heron has all but massacred them, though enough have always escaped to restock the pool with their offspring. Grass snakes also play havoc with the fish, though unable now to catch the larger individuals, which have reached portly dimensions. Foxes, hares and rabbits are often seen, but the badgers which have occupied their citadel in Oxpasture Wood for at least a century, apparently come up the hill only rarely, to excavate the wasp's nests in the bank of the ha-ha.

Starlings are the most compulsive bathers in our pond, flocks of them chattering like the urchins they are and scattering spray until every other bird in the garden feels compelled to join in the fun. Even the sedate song thrushes, which are modest bathers, come to stand deliberately within the arc of flying spray. Yellowhammers, linnets and goldfinches are also communal bathers whose flocks are frequent. Mallards come to feed on the pond weeds and the lapwings which nest on our meadows obviously enjoy bathing in the shallows. The pheasants and partridges, however, content themselves with dust-bathing among the azaleas.

Inside our window is a low bench seat, which is the favourite lookout and resting place of our poodle, who appears to enjoy the view from her level as much as we do from ours. For long periods she reclines with her tummy on the ledge and her hind-feet on the floor, silently watching the birds on the lawn with rapt attention. Thrushes, blackbirds and robins, which are always present, are permitted to come within a yard of the window without remonstrance, but the sight of a single pied wagtail, even if only balancing on a distant water-lily pad, sends her into paroxysms of excitement. For reasons known only to herself, she regards these dainty little birds, which run like clockwork mice across the grass, as a threat to our household. Until they are put to flight, she races up and down the window, barking furiously.

Looking out over the ever-changing panorama of the Sussex countryside, I like to imagine how it has altered over the centuries. This part of the county was once the southern border of the dense Wealden Forest, which divided the North and South Downs. Until the Romans built Stane Street and the London to Lewes road, the forest was a barrier to travellers and invaders alike and a region to be shunned as the haunt of savage wolves, bears and evil spirits. However, recent discoveries of pottery sherds in the Ashdown region suggest that Mezolithic hunters had at least temporary summer settlements in clearings burnt in the forest.

From 5000 B.C. to the coming of the Romans, human settlement was tied to the cultivation of the open hill-tops, the remainder of the land being either forest or swamp. The Sussex Downs, with their easily worked soil, were settled during the Neolithic Age, which left us its monoliths and stone circles. In the Bronze Age, the Beaker People introduced the first primitive foot-plough and began the long and ever-accelerating process of destroying the forests to make way for grazing animals. They left the Downs strewn with their tumuli and the pottery they discarded. The Iron Age men who followed them built great forts on the Downs and their iron implements are still being excavated today. Sussex was, of course, one of the great centres of the Iron Age civilization. With the coming of the Roman invaders came the wheeled plough, with coulter and curved iron blade, which could, for the first time, cut a deep furrow. Immediately the heavy clay soils of the valleys were exploited and the drainage of the great swamp-lands began. Permanent settlements began to appear in the valleys. Sussex is rich in disinterred Roman villas with exquisite mosaic floors and elaborate central heating systems. Not far from my house I watched the delicate work of excavating a Roman bath-house and marvelled that the lead drainage pipes were still in perfect condition after more than fifteen hundred years.

As the fertile valleys of Sussex came under cultivation, crops on the Downs were replaced by sheep-walks to support the thriving wool trade which the Romans soon established. But around A.D. 420, the Roman legions were finally forced to withdraw to the Continent. Britain, without the skilled if ruthless government of the Romans, speedily relapsed again into tribal warfare and disunity. Nevertheless, the face of Britain had been radically altered by the genius of the Roman road builders and engineers. When Ælle and his warrior sons Cymen, Wlencing and Cissa stormed the Sussex coast to herald the Saxon invasion in A.D. 477, they conquered an infinitely richer prize than had been won by the Roman legions five hundred years before. Although the spot where the Saxons landed on the Selsey peninsula has since been covered by the sea, we still have the ruins of Anderida, which we now call Pevensey, to remind us that this was where they massacred a Roman-British force.

Within a few miles of my house are the pre-Saxon burial grounds of Ringmer and Hassock. The gem-like Saxon churches of the Downs are tucked away in many a hidden valley. Judging by its name, Possingworth Park, where I live, was once a Saxon settlement. The name is clearly of Saxon origin and means 'the place of Possa's people'. Who, I wonder, was Possa? Does his ghost still stalk my beautiful valley, chasing the ghostly wild boar which have long since vanished from the land invaded by his people?

When the Norman William the Conqueror defeated the English pikemen in 1066, he chose Sussex as his landing place. The decisive battle of Hastings took place only eighteen miles from my window. Since then no foreign usurper has attempted to cross the English Channel, though both Napoleon and Adolf Hitler made elaborate plans to do so. Hitler did, however, leave his mark on Possingworth. Many bombs and several aircraft fell here and when the park was taken over by a Canadian armoured division for pre-D-Day battle training, it suffered severe devastation. Three years' work was needed to remove the litter of barbed wire and Nissen huts and to plant trees to hide the gun-sites and slit trenches. Even now I can watch great trees slowly dying from the concrete which was laid among them to enable squadrons of tanks to hide from spying eyes. However, as the years pass, nature is quietly healing these wounds suffered in a noble cause. One of our prized possessions is a group of beautiful Canadian maple trees, which were charmingly presented to us by Senator the Hon. Alan McNaughton, Speaker of the Canadian House of Commons, to commemorate the presence of his compatriots in the park during those anxious days.

To what better use can I devote my declining years than to plant trees which in the course of time add new beauty to this small corner of rural Sussex? Nothing gives me more pleasure than to watch their tender leaves unfurl just as the first willow warblers arrive from Africa to herald the spring with their delicate, cascading songs. Already many of the trees I have planted are thirty feet tall and of sturdy girth. The young maples are vivid with autumn colours and in snowy weather the berries of the mountain ashes attract flocks of hungry redwings and fieldfares. The graceful beeches, which are native to these parts and thrive in our acid soil, are becoming things of beauty even when leafless. But the slow-growing oaks, which, alas, are now so seldom planted, will still be saplings when I am no longer here to tend them. Nevertheless, I have planted hundreds of them, because there is no species which can match their biological importance to an English wood, nor which are so truly part of our natural heritage. I like to feel that when the noble park oaks, which are already well on in their second centuries, reach the end of their natural span, my contributions will replace them, to hold at bay the ever approaching ugliness of the modern world beyond. Who knows? Perhaps the stranger who will sit where I am now sitting, will be able to echo my belief that the view from my window is still as beautiful as can be seen anywhere in the length and breadth of England.

When Neil Armstrong, the first man on the moon, looked back on the blue planet Earth, he was deeply moved both by its beauty and by its smallness. All the astronauts have echoed his reflection that, viewed from outer space, man's only home in the vast universe seemed infinitely precious. 'But protection seems most required,' said Neil Armstrong, 'not from foreign aggressors or natural calamities, but from our own population.' If my travels around the world have taught me anything, it is the profound truth of this statement. We still have in our hands the power to protect the quality of life on earth, our precious space vehicle. If we are wise enough to use it, man's future can still be one of happiness and achievement. Though time is running out, I cling to my belief that wisdom will prevail. And I hope with all my heart that the lives of our future generations may be enriched by the beauties of the natural world as much as mine has been.

Appendix

Scientific names of animal species

In order not to clutter this book with too many tiresome specific names of species of animals, these are often referred to in general terms, *e.g.* parakeets, bats, etc. For the average reader these may be sufficiently self-explanatory. This appendix is for those interested in natural history who may require more precise information. It is divided into the mammals, reptiles and birds mentioned. Where exact names of species have been used in the text, *e.g.* Carolina Parakeet, the scientific name is given below. Trinomials are used only where subspecies are involved. Where only a general term has been employed, the scientific name of the Family or Genus is given. An indication of the range of the species or group of related species is also given, except in the case of birds, whose distribution, particularly of migrant species, is too complicated to be briefly summarized. For easy reference, the common names are listed alphabetically instead of in the correct scientific order.

MAMMALS

Addax *Addax nasomaculatus*   Sahara
Anoa *Anoa depressicornis*   Celebes
Ass, Wild (Onager) *Asinus hemionus*   Iran
Auroch *Bos primigenius*   Extinct
Baboon, Olive *Papio anubis*   Tropical Africa
Badger *Meles meles*   Europe, N. Asia
Bandicoots Peramelidae   Australia, New Guinea
Banteng *Bos banteng*   Java
Barasingha *Cervus duvauceli*   India, Nepal
Bats, Fox *Pteropus* spp.   S. Asia, Australia
  Fruit Pteropidae   Africa, Asia, Australia
  Painted *Kerivoula* spp.   S. Asia, New Guinea, Africa
Bear, Himalayan Black *Selanarctos thibetanus*   Himalayas
  Polar *Thalarctos maritimus*   Arctic
Bear, Syrian *Ursus arctos syriacus*   Asia Minor
Binturong *Arctitis binturong*   Assam to Borneo

Bison, American *Bison bison*   N. America
   European *Bison bonasus*   Only in zoos
   Jungle *see* Gaur
Blackbuck *Antilope cervicapra*   India, Pakistan
Blesbok *Damaliscus dorcas*   S. Africa
Boar, Indian Wild *Sus cristatus*   India
Bontebok *Damalescens pygargus*   S. Africa
Buffalo, African *Syncerus caffer*   Africa
   Indian *Bulbalus bulbalis*   S.E. Asia
Camel, Arabian *Camelus dromedarius*   N. Africa to India
   Bactrian *Camelus bactrianus*   Central Asia
Cat, Golden *Felis temminckii*   S.E. Asia
   Leopard *Felis bengalensis*   S. Asia, Indonesia, Philippines
Cheetah *Acinonyx jubatis*   Africa, Iran
Chinchilla *Chinchilla laniger*   Peruvian Andes
Chital *Axis axis*   India, Ceylon
Civet, African *Viverra civetta*   Africa
Colugo *Cyanocephalus variegatus*   S.E. Asia
Cuscus *Phalanger maculatus*   Celebes to Solomons
Deer, Axis *see* Chital
   Barking *Muntiacus muntjak*   S.E. Asia
   Fallow *Dama dama*   Mediterranean area
   Hog *Axis procinus*   India
   Mouse *Tragulus javanicus*   S.E. Asia
   Musk *Moschus moschiferus*   Himalayas, N.E. Asia
   Red *Cervus elaphus*   Europe
   Roe *Capreolus capreolus*   N. Europe, N. Asia
   Timor *Cervus timorensis*   Indonesia
Dingo *Canis* spp.   Australia
Dog, Hunting *Lycaon pictus*   Africa
Dugong *Dugong dugong*   E. Hemisphere warm coastal waters
Eland *Taurotragus oryx*   E. Africa
Elephant, African *Loxodonta africana*   Africa
   Indian *Elaphus maximus*   S.E. Asia
Fox *Vulpes vulpes*   N. America, Europe, Asia
   Arctic *Alopex lagopus*   N. Scandinavia to Canadian Arctic
   Bat-eared *Otocyon megalotis*   E. and S. Africa
Gaur *Bos gauris*   S.E. Asia
Gayal *Bos gaurus frontalis*   Bangladesh, Burma
Gazelle, Chinkara *Gazella gazella*   N. Africa, S. Asia
   Grant's *Gazella granti*   Africa
Genets *Genetta* spp.   S.W. Europe, Africa
Gerbils *Gerbillus* spp.   Africa, Asia
Goral *Naemorhedus goral*   Himalayas, S. China
Gibbons *Hylobates* spp.   S.E. Asia
Giraffe, Common *Giraffa camelopardalis*   Africa
   Masai *G. c. tippelskirchi*   Africa

Rothschild's *G. c. rothschildi*   Africa
Gnu, White-tailed   *Connochaetes gnou*   S. Africa (extinct in the wild)
Hare, Desert *Lepus arabicus*   Arabia, Baluchistan
    European *Lepus europaeus*   Europe, Asia
    Hispid *Caprolagus hispidus*   Assam, Nepal
Hartebeest, Jackson's *Alcelaphus lelwel*   E. Africa
Hippopotamus *Hippopotamus amphibius*   Africa
Hog, Giant Forest *Hylochoerus meinertzhageni*   E. Africa to Liberia
    Pygmy *Sus sylvanius*   Assam
Horse, Przewalski's   *Equus przewalskii*   Mongolia to Sinkiang
Hyena, Spotted *Hyaena hyaena*   E. Africa
Ibex, Himalayan *Capra sibirica*   C. Asia
Jackals *Canis* spp.   Europe, Africa, Asia
Jaguar *Panthera onca*   S. America
Jerboas Dipodidae   Africa, Asia
Kangaroos Macropodidae   Australia
Koala *Phascolarctos cinereus*   E. Australia
Kob, Uganda *Adenota kob*   Senegal to Uganda
Langur *see* Monkeys
Lemmings *Lemmus* spp.   Northern Europe, America, Asia
Lemurs Lemuridae   Madagascar
Leopard *Panthera pardus*   Africa, S. Asia
    Clouded *Neofelis nebulosa*   S.E. Asia
    Snow *Panthera uncia*   Himalayas
Lion *Panthera leo*   Africa
    Asiatic *P. l. persica*   Gir Reserve in India
Llama *Lama glama*   S. America (Extinct in wild)
Loris, Slow *Nycticebus coucang*   S.E. Asia
Lynx *Felis lynx*   Europe, Asia, Canada
Margay *Felis wiedi*   Mexico to Brazil
Markhor *Capra falconeri*   W. Himalayas
Monkey, Langur *Presbytis entellus*   S.E. Asia
    Proboscis *Nasalis larvatus*   Borneo
    Macaque *Macaca mulatta*   S.E. Asia, Japan
    Zanzibar Colobus *Colobus kirkii*   Zanzibar (Extinct?)
Mongoose *Herpestes* spp.   S. Europe, Africa, Asia
Ocelot *Felis pardalis*   S. America
Opossum, Leadbeater's *Gymnobelidius leadbeateri*   S.E. Australia
Orang-utan *Pongo pygmaeus*   Sumatra, Borneo
Oribi *Ourebia ourebi*   Africa
Oryx, Arabian *Oryx leucoryx*   Arabia
Otters *Lutra* spp.   Europe, Asia, N. America
Otter, Giant *Pteronura brasiliensis*   Amazon basin
    Sea *Enhydra lutris*   N. Pacific coasts
Panda, Giant *Ailuropoda melanoleuca*   Central China
    Red *Ailurus fulgens*   E. Himalayas, China
Pangolin, Malayan *Manis javanica*   India, Malaya
14

Pig, Bush *Potomochoerus porcus*   Africa
Puma *Felis concolor*   W. Canada to Patagonia
Quagga *Equus quagga*   Extinct
Rabbit, European *Oryctolagus cuniculus*   Europe, Africa, Australia
Rat, Giant *Cricetomys gambianus*   Tropical Africa
Reindeer *Rangifer tarandus*   Arctic Europe and Asia
Rhinoceros, African Black *Diceros bicornis*   Africa
   African White *Diceros simus*   Africa
   Great Indian *Rhinoceros unicornis*   N. India, Nepal
   Javan *Rhinoceros sondaicus*   Java
   Sumatran *Didermocerus sumatrensis*   Sumatra, Borneo, Burma, Malaya
Seal, Galapagos Fur *Arctocephalus galapagoensis*   Galapagos Is.
Sealions Otariidae   Pacific coasts
Serow *Capricornis sumatraensis*   E. Himalayas to Japan
Sheep, Blue (Argali) *Ovis ammon*   Central Asia
   Marco Polo's *Ovis ammon polii*   Pamirs
   Punjab Urial *Ovis orientalis punjabiensis*   Pakistan
   Shapu *Ovis orientalis vignei*   Caspian to Tibet
Shrew, Elephant *Rhynchocyon petersi*   E. Africa, Zanzibar
Springbok *Antidorcas marsupialis*   S. Africa
Squirrel, Giant Flying *Petaurista petaurista*   China, India, Indonesia
Squirrels Sciuridae   Europe, Asia, N. America
Suni, Zanzibar *Nesotragus moschatus*   Zanzibar (Extinct?)
Tahr, Himalayan *Hemitragus jemlahicus*   Himalayas
Tapir, Malayan *Tapirus indicus*   Malaya, Thailand, Sumatra
Tarsier *Tarsius bancanus*   Sumatra, Borneo
Thylacine *Thylacinus cyanocephalus*   Australia, Tasmania (Extinct)
Tiger, Balinese *Panthera tigris balica*   Bali (Extinct)
   Caspian *P. t. virgata*   Iran
   Chinese *P. t. amoyensis*   N.E. China
   Indian *P. t. tigris*   India, Bangladesh, Nepal, Bhutan, W. Burma
   Indo-Chinese *P. t. corbetti*   S. China to Malaya
   Javan *P. t. sondaica*   Java
   Siberian *P. t. altaica*   Soviet Far East
   Sumatran *P. t. sumatrae*   Sumatra
Vicuña *Vicugna vicugna*   N. Andes
Wallabies Macropodidae   Australia
Walrus *Odobenus rosmarus*   Arctic Atlantic and Pacific
Waterbuck *Kobus ellipsiprymnus*   E. and W. Africa
Whales Cetacea   World-wide
Wildebeest *Connochaetes taurinus*   Africa
Yak *Poephagus grunniens*   Tibet
Zebra, Burchell's *Equus burchelli burchelli*   Extinct
Zebra, Common *Equus burchelli*   Africa
   Mountain *Equus zebra*   Cape Province

REPTILES AND AMPHIBIANS

Cobra *Naja naja*   S.E. Asia
Crocodile African *Crocodilus niloticus*   Africa
   Asiatic *Crocodilus palustris*   S.E. Asia
   Estuarine *Crocodilus porosus*   S. Asia, Australia
Frog, Flying *Rhacophorus* spp.   Malaya, Indonesia
Gavial *Gavialis gangeticus*   S.E. Asia
Geckos *Gekko* spp.   World-wide
Iguana, Land *Conolophus subcristatus*   Galapagos Is.
   Marine *Amblyrhynchus cristatus*   Galapagos Is.
Lizard, Flying *Draco* spp.   S.E. Asia
   Lava *Tropidurus* spp.   Galapagos Is.
Monitor, Komodo *Varanus komodoensis*   Komodo Is.
Monitors *Varanus* spp.   Africa, Asia, Australia
Python, Rock *Python molurus*   S.E. Asia
Snake, Galapagos *Dromicus* spp.   Galapagos Is.
   Grass *Natrix natrix*   Europe
   Paradise Tree *Chrysopelea paradisi*   S.E. Asia
Tortoise, Aldabra Giant *Geochelone gigantea*   Indian Ocean Is.
   Galapagos Giant *Geochelone elephantopus*   Galapagos Is.
Turtle, Green *Chelonia mydas*   World-wide
   Hawksbill *Eretmochelys imbricata*   Bermuda to Brazil
   Leathery *Dermochelys coriacea*   Caribbean, S. Africa, Malaya

BIRDS

Albatross, Galapagos Waved
   Diomedea irrorata
Auk, Great *Penguinus impennis*
Avocet *Recurvirostra avosetta*
Babblers Timaliinae
Bee-eaters Meropidae
Bird-of-Paradise,
   Great *Paradisaea apoda*
   King *Cicinnurus regius*
Blackbird *Turdus merula*
Bluethroat *Erithacus svecicus*
Boobies *Sula* spp.
Brush-turkeys *Aepypodius* spp.
Bunting, Lapland *Calcarius
   lapponicus*
Bustards Otidae
Buzzard, Augur *Buteo rufofuscus*
   Rough-legged *Buteo lagopus*

Cassowary *Casuarius casuarius*
Chough, Alpine *Pyrrhocorax
   graculus*
Cockatoo, Palm *Probosciger atterimus*
   Sulphur-crested *Cacatua galerita*
Cockatoos Psittacidae
Cock-of-the-Rock *Rupicola peruviana*
Coot *Fulica atra*
Condor, Andean *Vultur gryphus*
Cormorant, Galapagos Flightless
   Nannopterum harrisi
Cormorants Phalacrocoracidae
Coursers *Cursorius* spp.
Crane, Common *Grus grus*
   Sarus *Grus antigone*
Cuckoo, Channel-billed *Scythrops
   novaehollandiae*
Darter, African *Anhinga rufa*
Dodo *Raphus cucullatus*

Partridge *Perdix perdix*
  Snow *Lerwa lerwa*
Peafowl *Pavo cristatus*
Pelicans Pelecanidae
Penguin, Adélie *Pygoscelis adeliae*
  Galapagos *Spheniscus mendiculus*
Petrels Procellariidae
Phalarope, Red-necked *Phalaropus lobatus*
Pheasant, Western Tragopan *Tragopan melanocephalus*
Pheasants Phasianidae
Pigeon, Comoro Blue *Alectroenas sganzini*
  Crowned *Goura cristata*
  Green *Treron* spp.
  Madagascar Green *Treron australis*
  Mauritius Pink *Nesoenas mayeri*
  Passenger *Ectopistes migratorius*
  Torres Strait *Myristicivora spilorrhoa*
Pigeons Columbidae
Plover, Blacksmith *Hoplopterus armatus*
  Golden *Pluvialis apricaria*
  Ringed *Charadrius hiaticula*
  Spurwing *Hoplopterus spinosus*
Quail, Rain *Coturnix coromandelica*
Quetzal *Pharomachrus moccino*
Redshank, Spotted *Tringa erythropus*
Redwing *Turdus musicus*
Robin *Erithacus rubecula*
Roller, Broad-billed *Eurystomus orientalis*
Sandgrouse Pteroclididae
Sandpiper, Wood *Tringa glareola*
Scrub-bird, Noisy *Atrichornis clamosus*

Shearwaters Procellariidae
Snipe *Gallinago gallinago*
Solitaires Raphidae
Sparrow, House *Passer domesticus*
Spoonbill, African *Platalea alba*
Starling *Sturnus vulgaris*
Stint, Temminck's *Calidris temminckii*
Stork, Marabou *Leptoptilos crumeniferus*
  Painted *Ibis leucocephalus*
  Whale-headed *Balaeniceps rex*
Sunbird, Purple *Nectarinia asiatica*
  Yellow-bellied *Nectarinia coquereli*
Sunbirds Nectariniidae
Takahe *Notornis mantelli*
Teal, Marbled *Marmaronetta angustirostris*
  Whistling *Dendrocygna* spp.
Tern, Noddy *Anous stolidus*
  Sooty *Sterna fuscata*
Thrush, Comoro *Turdus bewsheri*
  Dusky *Turdus obscurus*
  Laughing *Garrulax* spp.
  Song *Turdus philomelos*
  White's *Zoothera dauma*
Turaco, Schalow's *Tauraco schalowi*
Turnstone *Arenaria interpres*
Vulture, Himalayan Griffon *Gyps himalayensis*
  White-backed *Gyps bengalensis*
Wagtail, Pied *Motacilla alba*
  Yellow, *Motacilla flava*
Warbler, Radde's *Phylloscopus schwarzi*
  Willow *Phylloscopus trochilus*
Yellowhammer *Emberiza citrinella*

Index